CONQUER YOUR FEAR
OF THE
TRIATHLON SWIM

End the Dread!

M. ELLEN DASH
&
ALI MEEKS

Praise for *Conquer Your Fear of the Triathlon Swim*

"These concepts changed my life. As a fit athlete but a late-in-life swim competitor, I hit a wall with triathlons. This made me rethink my relationship with water—it changed everything! It felt like triathlon swim therapy: something I dreaded but then discovered was the best thing I ever did!" –**Triathlete E. Scott Osborne**

"The system of overcoming fear that Melon and Ali are teaching is second to none. Their message is spot on." –**Maryann Carrero, Triathlete and a graduate of Melon's program**

"This book is a fantastic resource for those suffering anxiety or panic attacks in the triathlon swim. Debunking the traditional 'tough it out' approach, *Conquer Your Fear of the Triathlon Swim* offers a strategic pathway to break free of a debilitating condition. Without doubt, it will improve the performance and quality of life of many." –**Triathlon Pro Coach Matt Koorey**

"VERY interesting. Coming from a sink or swim, 'tough it out' background, this was not at all what I was expecting. However, what a wonderful way to approach fear. I've always had a fear of jumping from extreme heights (typically into water). I always thought if I could start from a few feet, then gradually work up higher and higher, it would be easy and enjoyable. This book exemplifies that step-by-step approach. I LIKE IT!"
–**USA Triathlon Certified Coach Rick Greif**

"This book is chock full of excellent information: even if you're an experienced open-water swimmer or long-time triathlete, there's always something new to learn. As a fellow swim and triathlon coach, I found the book to be extremely helpful: I plan to use several of their tips with my own athletes. It's an excellent manual, and easy to read."
–**Swim/Tri and Leadership Coach Anne Duffy**

"Research shows that fear and lack of knowledge about open-water swimming can be two of the biggest barriers to entry in triathlon—but they don't have to be. *Conquer Your Fear of the Triathlon Swim* is a much anticipated resource for aspiring triathletes who are still in the process of finding comfort in open water. This book helps athletes see a path forward so they can chase their triathlon goals, no matter how big."
–USA Triathlon CEO Rocky Harris

Edited by Vince Font
Cover design by Dragan Lonchar
Published by Glass Spider Publishing
www.glassspiderpublishing.com

To my mother, who wasn't afraid.
She allowed me to try things most parents would shudder to watch.
She helped me learn to trust my body, a true gift.
Thanks, Mom.
—Melon Dash

To my mom and dad,
who took me to swim lessons and endured thousands of swim meets.
Thank you for your gift of a lifetime in love with the water.
—Ali Meeks

TABLE OF CONTENTS

ACKNOWLEDGEMENTS

A grand thank-you to all graduates of Miracle Swimming who have *so* inspired me and my staff for over 35 years! You have taught me how teaching and learning work, validated my conclusions, and spurred me to step out into the world and proclaim new truths that you experienced.

A second grand thank-you to all my licensees who came forward to learn to teach afraid adults, knowing we had the missing link.

Last but not least, thank you to Ali Meeks for writing down the bones of this book to get us started, and who provided the ever-ready fuel to ignite the next stage of the process. This was truly a team effort. Her tremendous grace to trust that in time it would come together, while I spent seven years slowly getting my part finished, made this possible. She practiced our mantra: go at your own pace and keep it fun.

–Melon Dash

First, I would like to thank the swimmers and triathletes of the world, including my own coached athletes at ReadySetSweat, who inspired me to write these words of hope. Thank you for letting me do this work I love.

Next, I'd like to thank the following people who contributed their prized time and energy to making this work a reality. My co-author Melon Dash is a talented writer, thinker, and friend who spent innumerable hours helping to shape this project. Rick Greif, Tony Alexander, Brenda Henderson, and Maryann Carrero gave to us their intensely personal experiences, and in doing so, helped our readers identify with the challenge of the triathlon swim. Your stories are important, and thank you for sharing them. Several incredibly busy people read and reviewed the book, providing priceless input and comments: Rick Greif, Laine Hendley, Tony Alexander, Scott Osborne, Rocky Harris, Matt Koorey, and Anne Duffy.

The talented cover designer Dragan Lonchar gave us a striking and sleek look for the book. Vince Font at Glass Spider Publishing was a professional and persevering project editor as he helped us craft and refine this product for you. We can't recommend him enough.

The generous and creative crew of Team Rocket Tri Club in Huntsville, Alabama gave brilliant feedback during our barrage of polls on book title and cover design. Team Rocket is an inspiration to athletes everywhere with their myriad of races and admirable group cohesion. Every city should be so lucky.

My non-triathlete husband Kelly Meeks endured oodles of insufferable conversations about the content and direction of this book. He deserves a tall tumbler of bourbon every time it is mentioned. And finally, my parents Elden and Diane Wick have been behind me all the way in everything I've ever done, no matter how crazy. Thank you all.

–Ali Meeks

PREFACE

Welcome, triathlon friends! Join us on this exploratory journey of triathlon swimming. The concepts in this book are a culmination of over 40 years of combined experience working and swimming with adults with fear of the water, whether in a pool, lake, or in beach conditions. With conviction, we bring you the most fundamental and far-reaching solution to overcoming fear in triathlon swimming.

Many of the issues triathletes experience are the same issues beginning swimmers have: anxiety, fear, and panic. The fear of panicking, not having fun, or not living through an experience is the beginning of panic. This is true whether you are learning to put your face in the water for the first time or swimming 2.4 miles in an iron-distance triathlon. You can't learn to swim if you're afraid you might not live. And you can't swim well in a triathlon if you're afraid you might panic.

For many years, swimming classes specially developed for afraid adults have been used to help them conquer their fear of water and learn to swim (www.miracleswimming.com). If the methods work for our Miracle Swimming students, then they will work for triathletes. We invite you into a circle of people who understand how the water works and how presence of mind is maintained. As a drop of water creates concentric ripples outward, we hope this book causes this circle of people to grow exponentially. May it take many with it as the expansion leads to every person in the world learning how to find their own safety in the water.

The authentic relationships we have with our athletes and students are encouraged between you and your coach. Almost everything we know about teaching and coaching swimming has been learned from our students and athletes. Find answers here that make sense to you. You already have much of the knowledge inside you. We hope the fun you have will cause the sport to not only grow, but become safer.

Let us know how you do.

Swimcerely,
Melon Dash and Ali Meeks, 2020

1

DO TRIATHLON SWIMS FREAK YOU OUT?

There is a very good reason why the swim is usually the first sport in a triathlon. Putting the swim first helps athletes draw on the fresh energy at the outset of the event to perform the swim and then move on to the other sports. But for many triathletes, the swim portion of a triathlon is a frenzied, blurry effort that ends not nearly soon enough. Before a triathlon, you may have been one of those who said, "I just have to get through the swim," or "I'll be fine once I get through the swim," or "I really love triathlon—except for the swim."

If you're an afraid swimmer, does it help to know that a whopping 46% of American adults are afraid in deep water in pools, and 64% are afraid in deep open water?[1] If you wouldn't characterize yourself as an afraid triathlete but would say you've experienced just a little fear or anxiety in triathlon swimming, it's important to recognize that fear is at the core. *And it's okay! It's also great information to know!*

---

[1] Gallup Poll, 1998.

How is it that I can bike a hundred miles, I can run a marathon, but I can't swim the length of the pool without being exhausted?

You can make progress if you know where you are and you start from there. But you can't make progress if you try to start from where you *aren't*. You may have felt a bit embarrassed or ashamed that you have not been able to overcome your fear of the swim. If so, you are in the good company of many, and this book is written for you.

You can *heal* your triathlon fear once and for all.

Meet Tony, Rick, and Brenda.

Tony's Story

"Telling my story is hard, because the way I was brought up, a guy is not supposed to feel panic. But obviously, we do.

I was brought up swimming in the Tennessee River, and I have been very comfortable in the water all my life. To this day I cannot understand why this panic experience happened. It is not only frustrating but it feels humiliating as well, since I have jumped out of airplanes and flown airplanes and done a lot of adventuring in my life, yet I have never panicked in those situations.

The race where the swim panic occurred was Wet Dog sprint triathlon in the Tennessee River (400-meter swim, 12-mile bike, three-mile run). I had done a few sprint triathlons before, and although I've always been slow and clumsy in the water, I had never felt panic. Leading up to this race, I had taken swim lessons and was able to swim over a mile wearing a snorkel. However, without my snorkel, I could never seem to breathe enough air, and so I was glad to find this race that allowed snorkels.

I remember thinking that the race would be such an easy breeze for me since I had trained so well and felt completely prepared. To this day, I do not understand why, but as soon as I got in the water and started the swim, I felt like I could not breathe. Almost immediately, my heart started racing and I started hyperventilating. I removed the snorkel and rolled over onto my back to swim on my back, but the feelings of panic would not go away. I remember being completely aware that this was a panic moment but felt powerless to stop it. It was so obvious that I was seriously struggling that a lifeguard stayed with me for the entire swim.

It was such a relief to finally finish the swim and get out of the water. I have never before or since experienced this type of panic. I don't know what I could have done differently to deal with this panic, or how I could have kept it from happening."

Rick's Story

"I've been competing in triathlons for 25 years and have completed over 250 triathlons. With that background, you wouldn't think I would have any open water issues, but I do. Don't get me wrong, I love swimming in open water. Anytime we go to the beach, that's where you'll find me. Despite all of that, I've had three complete freak-out moments in my long career.

My first panic occurred one cold, rainy morning during a half-iron distance race in Tennessee's Atomic Man Half-Iron distance race. The start had been delayed, and we all stood around shivering in waist-deep water waiting for the gun to go off. The race finally started and we took off in a frenzy. I was cold, stiff, and furious because I was repeatedly getting hit by the other swimmers. I remember feeling agitated and chilly when I suddenly felt my heart rate shoot sky-high. I tried to continue swimming, but by then I was in a full-blown panic.

For the first time in my life, I had to call a kayaker over to help me. A kayak quickly got to me, and I told the kayaker that I just needed to calm down and hang onto the kayak for a minute. I hung on, bewildered, and watched the next two waves of swimmers go by until I 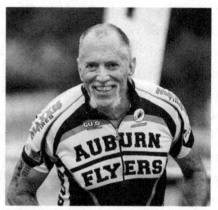 had settled down. Then, miraculously, I went on my way and had a great swim, a great race, and even pulled out a podium finish. I am not sure how I could have calmed myself down and relaxed other than stopping at that kayak, though, and I don't know what I would have done if he had not been there.

The next setting was at USA Triathlon Age Group Nationals in 2015 in Milwaukee, Wisconsin. I was in excellent shape and was looking forward to an exciting race. The water in Lake Michigan was very cold in the low 60's that day. It was a deep water start with athletes jumping in from the dock, and I sped off at the start in anticipation of a fast swim. Unfortunately for me, I hyperventilated again, feeling that familiar panic demon in my chest. I made my way to shallow water where I could stand and stood there until I settled myself down. I then continued on for a respectable yet far-from-podium finish. Once again, I'm not sure what I would have done if the bottom had not been there for me to stand on while I calmed down.

My most recent incident happened in 2017 at the Lake Placid, New York, half-iron distance race. This was my first long course race after having had a stem cell transplant and high dose chemotherapy for many months prior. My goal on this day was simply to finish the race, but the air temperature was very cold at 38 degrees, and the water felt freezing. When the race began, I was uncomfortably cold yet forging forward when all of a sudden my old panic showed up. Again this time, I flagged down and grabbed a kayak in order to get my breathing under control and continue the race.

I can see now that the common thread in all of these experiences is cold water. Even though now I try to think of the swim as a calm, smooth and easy warm-up, I still get anxious in cold water, and I feel that I don't have control when these panic symptoms start. It seems as though as long as the water is relatively warm, I can stay calm and all is good, but not in the cold. On the one hand, I feel like it is only a mental game, but on the other hand, I wonder what else there could be that could keep me from panicking in these situations."

Brenda's Story
"I'm an accomplished veteran in triathlon, but I still have fear in open-water swims. I can't understand why I've been able to do so much yet still worry about my safety. I've been a triathlete for over a decade in a number of distances in pools and open water, from

sprint all the way to iron-distance events. I've stood on the podium more than once in all kinds of races, and I've competed at the national and world championship level. Yet I still fear I'm not safe in deep open water.

Way back in my first triathlon, I ended up not finishing the swim because of fear. I think the reason I was afraid was that I was lacking experience and felt really inefficient in my stroke. In my next race, we were supposed to jump off of a dock to start the race. This terrified me because the water looked dark and very deep, and so I decided not to do the race.

Despite these experiences, I continued to train throughout that year, excited about the sport and encouraged by others around me. Thinking I had plenty of time to resolve my swim fear and feeling very fit, I decided to sign up for Ironman Florida the following year (2.4-mile swim, 112-mile bike, 26.2-mile run). It was a great year of training, but in the race swim I panicked due  to the ocean's swells and the inability to see well over them. I hadn't had much ocean swim experience, and the swells scared me. They still do.

Later that year, I completed a half-iron race in those same swell conditions, and although I was similarly terrified, I managed to overcome my fear by using a strong swim stroke and pushing through it. Two years later, I finished Ironman Florida again, feeling strong and finishing mid-pack, and felt great. I high fived everyone and had a great time in my best swim ever.

However, that feeling has been short-lived. After a couple of years off, I'm starting back to triathlons now, and I'm starting to feel that same fear creeping up. I worry that I won't be able to be safe in the water since I haven't practiced my open water swimming skills in a while and I'm not as strong as I was then. I wonder if my swim stroke would still be strong enough to save me, or if there is something else that makes me safe in deep water."

After reading these, you might be thinking, "Wow, that feels like something I could have written!" You may be frustrated with your swims and feel that they will never get better, like Tony. Maybe you push through your cold-water race anxiety, like Rick. You might have tried working on your freestyle technique to become stronger, like Brenda. And maybe, like all of them, you might wonder if the swim will always be scary, crazy, and difficult.

BUT GUESS WHAT? Swimming should not be scary, and there IS a way to make it comfortable. Cold water does not HAVE to trigger anxiety. **A better freestyle stroke is not the answer.** There is a better way to approach swimming, and here's the point at long last:

Being able to swim freestyle is not the same as knowing how to swim.

You may be saying, "Wait, what? Are you saying that if I know how to do freestyle and tread water, I may not know HOW TO SWIM?"

Yes!

Well, then, what is "being able to swim?" Being able to swim is being confident, calm, in control, and safe in water that is over your head. Being able to do strokes is knowing how to swim *efficiently*.

There are two legs on which safety stands: presence of mind and understanding of how the water works. Right now, if you have fear in the water, you're missing one or both of those legs! But recall what Captain Marvel used to say in those 80s afterschool commercials you may have seen: "Knowing is half the battle!" Now, let's win the battle.

What does NOT being able to swim look like? It looks like fearful stroking and treading that saps your energy, destroys your endurance, and causes uncertainty, worry, and puts you in danger. It also takes the fun out of the swim. When you get tired and are at the end of your energy, stroking and treading are not the answer. The real key to knowing how to swim (whether you're participating in a triathlon or otherwise) is being in control. When there is control, there is no fear in the first place. This fear can be healed with an understanding of how your body works in the water and how to keep your presence of mind so that you can maintain control. You need to stand on both of these "legs" to *feel* safe and *be* safe in a triathlon.

You are on your way to making the swim the best part of the triathlon by healing your fear once and for all.

2

UNPACKING FEAR OF TRIATHLON SWIMS

You've already made it through the hard part, which is deciding to take a closer look at the anxiety you may have faced or recognized in your triathlon swims. Welcome to the easy part! Whether you know it or not, you are on the verge of a revolution in changing the way you experience triathlon swimming.

2.1   Why the swim is often feared and despised

Do most triathletes despise the swim portion of the race? In our experience, yes. Their sentiment is understandable for several reasons.

2.1.1   Panic

Let's get the obvious one out of the way right now! Lots of people experience what they would term "panic" in a triathlon for a number of reasons. They may have feelings of intense worry, tightness in the chest, shortness of breath, and racing heartbeat, all of which feel terrible.

Panic not only feels dangerous, it *is* dangerous. Recent research has confirmed this:

"There are few studies to draw from which examine fear of water and drowning. Harris et al. (2010) found that swimming deaths among triathletes were attributed to panic. Deaths were most often in high density triathlons that began with open-water simultaneous starts involving many novice competitors. In these cases, distressed athletes were not identified and timely resuscitation not performed." *(From the doctoral dissertation, Haynsworth, Nancy M. An Action Research Approach to Fear as an Impact on Water Safety Outcomes Among African Americans in South Carolina.)*

Just because panic *has* been part of your triathlons in the past doesn't mean panic must be part of them going forward.

2.1.2   Other fear-related reasons

- ○ **Oxygen deprivation.** A lot of people entering the sport of triathlon don't have a swimming background or don't swim consistently. Once they start swimming more, they find they don't know how to breathe while swimming. And it's hard to swim if you don't have enough air! In addition, lack of air makes you feel anxious and panicky.

- ○ **Wetsuit drama.** Many triathlon fears can be triggered by wetsuits, especially if they haven't been worn regularly in training but brought out the morning of the race. The tight neck and chest in the wetsuit can cause you to feel like you can't breathe well, and the strange buoyancy afforded by the neoprene can make you feel off balance. In addition, wetsuits are normally worn in colder-water races, and the shock of cold water to the face (and arms, if it's sleeveless) can result in restricted blood flow to the limbs and organs that makes you feel short of breath. These feelings of tightness, restricted breathing, and chilliness can lead to fear sensations.

o **Deep-Water Blues.** The next and biggest reason the triathlon swim is feared is that it involves deep, open water, which is scary for many people. Not being able to touch the bottom sends many into a panic. If you are afraid you might not live, you won't swim well.

2.1.3 Reasons unrelated to fear

o **You'd rather be biking.** Another reason the triathlon swim is ill-loved is that swimming spans the shortest amount of time in triathlons relative to the other sports, and the bang-for-the-buck factor seems low in terms of time spent training swimming. Often, the swimming that does take place consists of a few random swims squeezed into a busy biking and running schedule. On race day, athletes just hope for the best since swimming seems to be the least important part of the race. However, the shortness of the triathlon swim disguises the tiredness it produces. Even though the swim is short, if it's the weak link in your race and a sore point with your anxiety and fear, you start the race already exhausted and unhappy.

o **Swimming seems like a hassle.** For some people, swimming is a production. It can take a lot of time to get to the pool, get your gear ready, complete the workout, wash the chlorine off, dry off, and go home. Not having the right equipment is a recurring issue, and once in the pool, the activity can seem quite boring. Not only that, but swimming is a challenge to fit into a busy day, and pool hours are often restrictive.

It's great to want to do triathlons. The fact people are willing to struggle as much as they do during the swim just to participate is amazing. Clearly, you are committed! However, your safety is at stake. It's not worth risking! And much more fun can be had if you approach it correctly.

Where does this leave you? It leaves you understanding the main reason why swimming is so often hated in triathlon: **people are afraid that they'll panic, that they'll look silly or feel terrible, and that they might not live.**

2.2   Knowing how to swim means what, exactly?

There are shelves of books and countless articles dealing with the fear of open-water swimming. You may have read all of these but are wondering why you still have a problem. The answer is that you may have been working on a better stroke technique and better conditioning—but these are not the solution to fear. They are unrelated to healing fear. To say goodbye to fear of the triathlon swim, we need to go back to basics you may have skipped without realizing it.

2.2.1   What is the definition of knowing how to swim?

In the Vietnamese language, there is only one word for both *blue* and *green*. To denote *green*, you say one variation of *xanh*, which means "tree blue." To denote *blue*, you say the other variation of *xanh*, which means "sky blue." But you can also just say "xanh" and the context of the sentence will clarify what you mean. Similarly, our culture uses the word *swimming* in many ways, such as "knowing how to swim," "I can swim," "she is swimming," and

"I'm going swimming"—some of which mean different things to different people. The definition of "I can swim" or "knowing how to swim" is critical, because it's the difference between success and failure—even life and death.

Let's say you have a friend who grew up with parents who took him to the pool when he was young, and the three of them played together. At an early age, his parents passed him between them in the water so he could learn that it held him up and how it worked. Then, say by age two, he could move from here to there on his own, come up for air when he needed it, and by age three he could turn onto his back to rest. His movements were probably fast, his fingers were apart, and he held his breath most of the time, but it worked. He felt safe, and he liked being in the water. He felt the water holding him up; he could propel himself, and he was in control of getting air.

His mom may have said to her friends at a play date, "Johnny can swim! I mean, he can't *swim*, but he can swim!" The mom is referring to two things. But she's using the same word. Johnny knows how the water works and has become independent for short periods of time. He can "Swim." But he doesn't know formal strokes like freestyle or backstroke yet; he can't "swim." The capitalized "Swim" gets prominence for its meaning of safety. To be able to Swim requires two things: knowing how the water works, and being in control of getting air. The non-capitalized "swim" means strokes. Strokes provide efficiency, but they do not provide safety. By efficiency, we mean greater distance per stroke and less energy output for a given a distance.

The point of learning to Swim is safety: the ability to rely on yourself for your safety in water over your head. The point of learning to swim (stroke) is to be efficient, to get exercise, to swim faster or further, to win races.

Strokes do not make you safe.
They *do* help you finish a triathlon sooner.

Strokes are merely the choreography[2] of swimming for efficiency's sake. Once a person learns to Swim (safety), then s/he can learn to swim (be efficient). Did you try to learn to be efficient before you learned to be safe? You're not alone. It seems everybody's doing it!

Do you know that the water holds you up? Have you ever been completely still in shallow water to find out? Did your feet sink? If so, did your face also go to the bottom? Do you know what floating means?

The definition of knowing how to Swim and being a Swimmer—to us—is confidence, therefore achieving comfort and safety in the water, no matter the depth or race length or aggressiveness of the competitors. You can take care of yourself in the crowd and remain in control. When you can rely on yourself for your safety, you no longer have a reason to panic, and you no longer have to manage your fear. It is healed.

2.2.2   Not Drowning
Let's get this mysterious subject out of the way. What is drowning? In lay terms, it's suffocation caused when water prevents air from getting to the blood. One way that air is prevented from reaching

---

[2] Strokes as the choreography of swimming is an idea advanced by instructor Christopher Canaday.

the blood is if water enters the furthest reaches of the lungs—the alveoli—blocking oxygen from passing from the alveoli to the blood. It's not easy for water to reach the alveoli, or for the airway to become blocked. When a person is afraid or is struggling at the surface, that person is *not* close to drowning. But fear can lead to panic, which is the biggest danger. In panic, people can hold themselves unwittingly below the surface. Note: The biggest danger is not the inability to do freestyle or tread water. It's the inability to remain present. And hey, good news—this ability to remain present can be learned, and it is the main reason we wrote this book.

To drown because of fear, a person has to: 1) not know how the body and the water work together; 2) struggle in the water to the point of exhaustion; 3) let go of one's buoyancy (unless a person has none, in which case, go directly to #4—but most people are buoyant); 4) drop below the surface and not maintain the presence of mind to return to it; 5) not be able to withstand the feeling of being near the end of the breath without panicking; 6) remain underwater longer than the breath lasts; 7) panic; and 8) give up. In other words, a lot has to go wrong in order to drown.

Preventing drowning is made virtually certain when you understand how your body and the water work together, and you know how to prevent panic. These are easy to learn once you know the steps. It takes most people a couple of weeks of focused practice to learn what's needed. It may be the best training time you ever spend. It makes more sense to handle these lessons before working on swimming conditioning. Get the basics first.

If you are calm, you can be in the water with little effort. If you are not calm but afraid, you struggle, which makes it difficult to breathe easily. This begets more fear. Fear and panic have no place in the triathlon swim.

3

FEAR-FREE SWIMMING FOR ALL

There are three things you can do with fear: avoid it, manage it, and heal it.

Avoidance works, but then you don't get to do the sport you love. Management is another tactic: "I need to train harder! I need to fix my stroke technique. I need to learn anxiety-reduction techniques." However, managing fear in a swim could be unsafe. Even more so, when managing their fear, people often still hate the swim. Why? Is there something wrong with the swimmers and coaches? No. It's just that big information is missing with regard to healing fear for good.

That said, there are times in life when managing our fear—pushing through it—is sufficient, like being nervous on a first date or cooking dinner for a new friend. But if managing didn't work at those times, it wouldn't be life-threatening. When our lives are on the line, healing it is the best (and only) long-term solution.

Do you believe you can heal your fear? Just because you've tried and it didn't work doesn't mean you're sunk. It just means it's time to use the right tools for the job.

Start with the time-honored paradigm that life and sport coaches far and wide have come to use: BE→DO→HAVE.

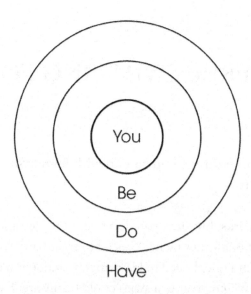

This means that if you "BE" something, only then can you "DO" something, and only then can you "HAVE" the thing that comes from the being and doing. The world makes the most sense when BE→DO→HAVE are in that order. We can't switch around the having with the doing and the being. Make sense? Well, if not, don't worry—that's pretty abstract for us, too! Let's look at some examples.

Suppose you wanted to HAVE a real working police car. We all know that you can't just HAVE a real working police car. You have to *BE* a police officer in order to *DO* police work and *HAVE* a real police car. You can't just DO driving around in a police car without BEing a police officer (unless you want to go to jail). Another example of what it would be to try to put the HAVE first:

suppose you wanted to HAVE a job as a sign language translator. You can't DO sign language translation unless you ARE a sign language translator. You have to BE someone fluent in sign language so that you can DO the sign language translation and then you can HAVE the job. It has to be in the order of BE→DO→HAVE.

Relating this to swimming, if you are *BEing* calm, you can *DO* calm in the water in order to *HAVE the effects of being calm*. Once you can BE calm, you can HAVE safety, whether you are in a pool or in deep, open water.

You may have thought it worked this way:
If I HAVE a skill of freestyle, I will be able to DO— propel myself efficiently—and then I'll BE a swimmer.

That would be HAVE→DO→BE.

You have tried developing the skill. You have performed strokes. But you have not become a Swimmer—someone who is comfortable and safe in deep water. As you can see, HAVE→DO→BE is not the way it works, and it's not the solution. Strokes don't make you safe or confident. Nor does improved stroke technique. Nor does more conditioning. Someone who can Swim is not afraid in deep water.

3.1   The Habit of Jumping from Calm to Fear

The next thing to learn is how to be calm in the swim, and what the sport of triathlon can be when you achieve this calm. To start that journey, let's talk about what calm and fear look like in a new way.

3.1.1 Calm to Panic: The 5 Circles

If you want to develop expertise in being calm and in control, you have to practice being calm and in control. We know you'll be excited at your race. But being relatively calm while also being excited implies that you feel safe. Starting and staying safe so that you can feel calm is the foundation of swimming without fear. What would you need to do in order to be calm? How far "back" do you need to go? Go there.

Have you ever arrived at work and forgotten how you got there? Where were you when you were driving? Your body was in the seat but your thoughts and your mind were elsewhere.

Have you ever hit your thumb with a hammer? Closed your fingers in the car door? Cut your finger with a knife in the kitchen? These were times when you weren't all "there." You can be somewhere else because there are two parts of you: a physical part and a non-physical part.

The part of you that comes and goes from your body is your non-physical self. We call it *you*. You can be present and "mindful," or you can be absent and "gone" . . . or somewhere in between.

Everyone knows what it means to be not really "there" when someone is talking to you, for example. When you forgot to close your gas cap, where were you? It's not that you're an idiot, it's that you were somewhere else. Your presence was missing.

Being present is a prerequisite to being in control. And if you're not in control, how can you improve?

How does being calm work? How do you stay calm? The story begins where all great stories begin: with a picture! (Figure 3.1.1)

Figure 3.1.1. The 5 Circles: Universal Steps of Panic ©M. Dash 1983.

In this graphic, the stick figure represents your body, and the circle represents your non-physical self. This diagram shows the process of moving from comfort to panic as the non-physical self moves out of the body (See Figure 3.1.1).

The 1st Circle represents a place where the physical and non-physical self are together, and you feel calm, comfortable, peaceful, centered, grounded, and in control: the state of being "at home." This is the state of mindfulness or presence.

The 2nd Circle is where you and your body have begun to separate. Mindfulness is decreasing. You might say you have cold feet, feel weak in the knees, or there's a question in the air: you're nervous. You may actually have fun doing some activities in the 2nd Circle, such as roller coasters or haunted houses. Note, however, that it's fun being in the 2nd Circle in some situations, but it's not so fun being in the 2nd Circle in water where you're not sure of your safety.

The 3rd Circle is where fear feels like fear, where feet and hands feel clammy and you have butterflies in the stomach. You're thinking, "This is not fun. Get me out of here!"

The 4th Circle is the state when you're scared stiff: you're completely paralyzed by fear and cannot move. This is dangerous.

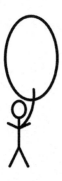

The 5th Circle represents abject panic, where you have lost it, are "freaked out," and are not in control of when, how, or if you come back to control. You're not dead; there's still a thin thread of energy connecting you to your body. But you're not mentally there. As you know, it takes no time at all to go from the 1st Circle to the 5th Circle when you feel very unsafe.

For those who are unfamiliar with this 5 Circles diagram and the "Miracle Swimming"[3] method, this method has been used for over 35 years to teach beginning swimming to thousands of adults who are afraid in water. It is the most powerful, effective, and reliable method for teaching people with fear of water that we've seen. Some of its graduates had terrible, heart-wrenching experiences in water, or had parents who never learned to swim, or avoided water due to family or cultural constraints. Some simply never had water access. Miracle Swimming is virtually 100% successful. You can be 100% successful, too.

Who is in control of which circle you are in? Right: YOU ARE! When you learn to swim comfortably in the way described in this

---

[3] www.miracleswimming.com

book, you do not have to go to the 2nd, 3rd, 4th, or 5th Circles, ever again. You can stay in the 1st Circle and do everything you need to do to be a successful triathlon swimmer in every race.

How do you stay in the 1st Circle, then? You do this by backing up all the way to the place where you can be comfortable, in the pool or open water. Is that on the beach? Is it standing in shallow water? Wherever you are, start and stay there and move slowly into the exercises described in this book without ever leaving the 1st Circle. Go *slowly*. Be attentive (present) to your sense of safety, not progressing to the next skill unless you're completely comfortable. It's more advanced to repeat something and stay in the 1st Circle than it is to move to the next stage and be in the 2nd Circle. You will thus move most efficiently in small, reliable, certain steps to total comfort in deep and open water. How would it feel to stop worrying and pushing yourself? Give yourself a chance to learn this the correct way so you can enjoy the water for the rest of your life. The only way to *become an expert at being calm is to practice being calm*. You do not need to be any better at being nervous or afraid!

You might insist, "But seriously, isn't the answer to conquering my triathlon swim fear facing my fear head on and practicing what makes me afraid?"

_No!_ Facing fear does not have to be threatening. *Healing fear cannot be threatening*. It's possible to heal a lifelong fear without being scared. In coping with fear, you have a choice to either avoid it, manage it, or heal it. If you're afraid, you have likely been managing it. You've found that managing it isn't satisfying, so you're reading this book. You're afraid in deep or open water, and you know that's unsafe. If it's not the depth or open water that's scary to you but rather the crowd and how people act sometimes, we'll talk about that later.

3.1.2   Panic

Do you know anyone terrified of deep, open water who has tried to manage their fear by doing more open-water swimming? It's commonplace. Did they get over it? Probably not. By continuing to do open-water swims while afraid, they spend a lot of time in the 3rd Circle, which is far closer to the 5th Circle than the 1st Circle. This is not only dangerous, it's misguided. Is this person safer now? No. The fear is still there. When something happens out of the ordinary—a wave hitting the face, a crowded buoy, or becoming exhausted—the managed fear comes out of hiding. Meet the 5th Circle: panic! Fear and panic are key reasons that many triathletes feel unsafe in the water[4]. Panic is dangerous. Fear is also dangerous, especially if you don't know how to return to the 1st Circle.

These triathletes are indeed unsafe because they lack key information. The belief that they are unsafe causes movement from the 1st or 2nd Circle to the 5th. Panicking doesn't make them safer, but rather makes the situation more dangerous—they are not in control of themselves.

Panic is the playing out of a habit you've unconsciously learned.

---

[4] Understand that "panic disorder, " according to the National Institute of Mental Health (NIMH), is an anxiety disorder which causes sudden, repeated, and unpredictable fear attacks with no obvious trigger that last for several minutes. We are not talking about this disorder; we are talking about a panic feeling triggered by a belief that we're unsafe in the water. (NIMH is the lead U.S. federal agency for research on mental health disorders.)

It's not something to blame yourself for; we all have habits about one thing or another (or more likely a handful of things), and we came upon them honestly. When the going gets really rough, we "leave" our bodies and go to the 5th Circle (panic) to get away from the distress. Either we regain control and remove ourselves from the situation, or someone else does. Truthfully, we have every right to leave. But it makes matters worse.

The first time the going got this rough, the pain you endured was so bad you decided, consciously or not, that you never wanted to feel that way again. So, if a similar situation came along again, your new mechanism was to leave (panic) and prevent the awful feeling. It's completely understandable. The dangerous thing, though, is that you are not in control. You can't take care of your body. This is how we humans cope . . . until we realize how putting ourselves in a potentially panic-inducing situation is perilous.

Before panic happens (5th Circle), you get many warning signals. You may think triathlon swim panic happens out of the blue, but there are almost always precursors. For example, you have an inkling that you don't want to do the swim with everyone else, but you dismiss it and do it anyway.

At that juncture you had a choice between doing the pragmatic thing (going through with it) or the thing you wanted to do (not swim), and you chose the pragmatic thing. But why not give yourself what you really want? It keeps you in your body . . . .as in "alive!"

What are the messages your body gives you?

3.1.3 Hyperventilation

If you don't honor your body's warning signals, it will start to communicate in a way that you can't help but hear. Hyperventilating is one of those ways. This is a built-in system to keep you safe. Will you honor it, or dismiss it? If you dismiss it, panic is a way for your body to begin screaming.

To prevent panic and hyperventilating in swimming, listen to your body. Stay in the 1st Circle. You can learn to stay in 1st Circle by backing up to a place where you are completely comfortable and beginning to learn again from there. But this time the goal will be the 1st Circle, not a swim technique movement.

3.2   Staying Calm

To learn to stay calm, promise yourself that you'll keep yourself feeling safe at all times. By learning while you feel safe, you stay in control. Recall the diagram:

©M. Dash 1983. Stay in control—the 1st Circle—to stay safe.

Learning happens when we feel safe.
Healing fear happens when we feel safe.
Healing fear is finished when you
feel safe all the time.

The more in-control of yourself you are, the more you can do. The more you can do, the more desirable experiences you'll have (BE→DO→HAVE). By practicing only what you can do while feeling in control and therefore calm, you build trust in yourself, fear melts, and confidence grows. You become eager to try things in a new way. They work. It has worked in teaching thousands of adults with a crippling fear of the water, and it will work for you. It cannot possibly fail . . . unless you don't use it.

Speaking of teaching, around the turn of the 1900s there lived an Italian teacher and researcher named Dr. Maria Montessori. You may recognize this name as a type of school in which experiential or hands-on learning is employed to teach children, and indeed these schools are named after her. What you may not know about Montessori's wildly successful teaching philosophy and technique is that her system is predicated upon her belief in the child's natural curiosity to learn.

Dr. Montessori believed that the innate curiosity children possess would drive them to solve life's most difficult puzzles. She believed children are driven to learn by this interest, and that they will inevitably reach toward knowledge and find it at the right time for them. This search for learning extends to adulthood and beyond, into the rest of life.

While you may be saying, "Are you kidding me? I hated school!" think about the fact you probably have a hobby or two you've sought information about, and at which you've become proficient—like cooking, car repair, or triathlon. So even if you are the most hardened of formal-education haters, you have no doubt retained vestiges of your preschool self.

Relating this tendency to swimming, by practicing and mastering something that allows you to stay calm, you will naturally and inevitably want to know the next thing. Once that next thing is learned while being calm, the following thing will become more apparent. As you do this, you become more and more comfortable in the water and your skills expand. You build trust in yourself. The result is that you learn to trust yourself 100% in the water. This is a very happy place, indeed.

What is it that you need to practice and master? It's being "in your body" in water, the 1st Circle—not having your body here and you over there, or being in the past thinking about what happened last time, or in the future thinking of what might happen next. When you're in the present, you are in your body, and when you are in your body, you are in control.

This control isn't limited to the water. Learning to be in your body can impact all parts of your life, once you learn how. Wouldn't it be great if one of the benefits of triathlon was that you learned how to be more present in all aspects of your life? It's something to think about. Meanwhile, let's discuss what it actually means to be in control.

3.2.1 Doing Skills Versus Being in Control
Which is more important: being in control, or performing a skill?

You may know the answer by now, at least in theory. Think about someone who is uncomfortable putting their face in the water. If this person had to put their face in the water in order to learn to swim, they'd be practicing the 3rd Circle, which is no fun. Intuitively, you know this is wrong. It's more important for them to be in control and feel good than it is for them to complete the skill and resist (hate?) it.

You're reading this book because you want to be in control in water—shallow or deep, open water or pool—whether someone splashes you, jumps in right next to you, bumps into you, or if you step off an underwater ledge or fall from a dock or boat. True? Control only comes by practicing control. Learn it in steps.

3.2.2   Tension as Communication

When your body is tense, you're receiving a message from your beliefs that you are not safe. It would be unwise to proceed if you actually aren't safe. The part of you that believes you're not safe is the part of you that is learning and overcoming fear. To overcome fear, you must pay attention to that tension. When you're listening to your body, you feel safer. When you let tension be there, it gradually disappears. Your belief starts to change. Your trust in yourself grows. Listen to your body; it's the communication channel between your wisdom and you.

Have you ever been told by swimming teachers and family members to relax in the water? Being told to relax is practically a joke for someone who is afraid. If you try to make tension disappear ("RELAX!"), it usually persists. As the saying goes: "What you resist persists."

You don't want to be tense, since tension means you're not having fun and you're in the 2nd or 3rd Circle. At the same time, you don't want to tell yourself to relax because it's not a reliable solution. Sometimes it works, and sometimes it doesn't.

At this moment it would be too scary to be in the middle of a triathlon swim, feel panicky, and let yourself be panicky. We are not asking you to do that. Instead, learn the basics of how the water works in the pool far from a triathlon so you can embody this infallible system in a safe place without pressure.

You need a system that gives you the best chance of staying in control or regaining control every single time. The system to learn is this:

Let yourself be the way you are.

By going slowly and letting yourself be tense, if you truly allow it, your tension goes away. This is a most effective solution, and it heals fear.

If at some time in the future you find yourself in a frightening situation and you cannot make yourself relax, you will still be able to pull through because you will have developed a far more dependable habit: letting yourself be the way you are. When you practice this, you allow what's already happening to happen, and you will automatically begin to relax. Tension is okay, and your trusting it will heal it. Don't be in a hurry to change. The change will happen on its own, naturally, when you're in your body. Change doesn't happen if you're pushing.

3.2.3   Not Comparing Yourself to Others

To compare yourself to others, or to compare yourself to your vision of where you "should be," is to be outside of yourself—looking back at yourself. This is outside the 1st Circle. Being outside of your body, you're in no position to learn. You may even be in a criticizing position, ready to judge yourself if you don't measure up to someone else. Is this going to help you learn? If you're comparing yourself to others, bring yourself back into your body and feel your feelings. Impatience? Sadness? Tension? Hurry? Just be still and feel them. They have a place in your learning and healing. Just feel as much as you feel safe to feel. Let that emotion be there. This is allowing healing.

When you recover from comparing yourself, consider doing something in the pool that makes you feel safe. When you're ready to try it, go slowly, the safest way. Feel. Feel what it's like to be in the exact same place your body is, to fill your body with your presence from head to toe, fingertip to fingertip. If you do this, you're likely to feel the water in a way you haven't felt it before. You may feel your buoyancy. Sometimes people feel the resistance of the water, which is so much greater than that of air. Sometimes people feel how their balance is different than on dry land. All these are factors to learn about. You can learn about these because you feel safe. That is what matters. Fun matters, too, but you have to feel safe in water to get there.

3.2.4   No Such Thing as Stuck

All things in the universe are composed of energy in one form or another: your body, your thoughts, light, sound, information, emotion. Energy does only two things. It expands and contracts. Everything in the universe expands and contracts. Though you may not be able to detect it, your chair expands and contracts in a rhythm of its own. So do the molecules of this page. And though we don't yet have instruments sophisticated enough to measure them, your moods and your learning expand and contract in their own rhythm. You may say, "I understand that energy expands and contracts. But I have also felt stuck. Isn't that a third thing energy does?" No. "Stuck" can only happen if there's contraction. Energy keeps expanding unless there's contraction.

Contraction is part of the cycle of learning. It's not bad. It just is. We contract when it's necessary to "keep ourselves safe" according to our beliefs. Keeping yourself safe keeps you in your body, which is a healing step.

How does this relate to your swimming? When you're in the water and you're worried, how does your body feel? It contracts—gets tense. Your chin may come down, your shoulders may hunch up, your breathing may get shorter and quicker, and your chest, throat, arms, legs, and jaw may tighten.

On the other hand, when you feel safe in the water, how does your body feel? You're relaxed, expanded. You feel looser, more at ease. You expand your body by thinking calming, soothing thoughts. You contract by thinking scary, threatening thoughts.

You may have never thought of having control over what thoughts you had in the water. And you may not have had any control. But today, open yourself to this possibility: when you're on land and you notice yourself having scary thoughts and tensing up, check your thoughts. Are those the thoughts you want to have? If yes, fine. If no, fine. Are they based in truth? If yes, fine. If no, fine!

Just be aware that you have a choice.

We are not asking you to talk yourself out of fear. We are simply asking you to acknowledge your thoughts.

Once you do that, come back to your body and feel what it's telling you. Honor its instructions. The solution that works is slowing down and making sure you're taking care of yourself in this moment.

3.2.5 Stay in Your Body

Where you are now? Are you in your body? Are you partly in your body and partly somewhere else? Are you totally "gone?" No. You'd have to reread the paragraph if you were gone. Here's a useful exercise. You can record it on your phone and play it back:

- o Bring your focus into your body fully. Feel what it's like to be totally "home." Is this where you spend most of your day? Part of your day? Any of your day? (Just kidding.)
- o Now close your eyes and feel yourself sitting in your seat. Be "home." Be aware of your sitting position, the clothes you're wearing, the way they feel on your body, and your sensations.
- o Now pretend you're across the room looking back at your body. It's sitting in the chair. See the position it's in and what it's wearing.
- o Then, bring yourself back into your body again. You're home again. How does it feel?
- o Now imagine yourself again across the room, looking back at your body sitting in the chair. Look at it from across the room.
- o Now return to your body again and feel what it's like to be in it. It feels different to be in your body than to be across the room. Did you feel it? This is a good exercise to teach

you the different feelings between being in your body, and being out of it. Don't worry if you were not able to do it. Not everyone can do this.

When you're in the water, you can keep your energy in your body by feeling. Feel how the water embraces every inch of your body. Feel how it buffets you ever so slightly, back and forth, or holds you as you simply stay still. Feel your arms' lightness in the water. Feel how much air you have in your lungs. By keeping your attention (your focus, yourself) in your body, you remain in the present, in control. It's simple. It works.

For those challenged by the message about being in your body, here is one student's comment: "It sounds like (a bunch of hooey), but it works." —Tim

3.3   How Long Does It Take to Learn?
Learning to swim involves learning to listen to your body in the water. This learning has a timetable that is all its own. It involves taking a look at what caused you to have trouble in the past.

3.3.1   Your Timetable
There is a key decision you must make before moving forward. Are you willing to make your first and highest priority staying in the 1st Circle, in control? When you put the 1st Circle first, you give yourself permission to do what sounds like fun. You will make progress, and you will learn. Can you place a checkmark here?

____ My top priority is feeling safe in the water. To feel safe, I must be in control of myself.

48

So rather than practicing fear, every time you look at a new step in learning, whether it's putting your face in the water or swimming out into deep ocean water, ask yourself, "Do I want to do this? Does this sound like fun? Can I stay in 1st Circle for it?" If not, in order to heal your fear, take a step backward and **don't allow yourself to move forward until you can stay in the 1st Circle.** Going backward is going forward. More than thirty-five years of 100% success have proven this teaching.

You may be thinking, "Oh, no, I may have to slow down!" This is an understandable concern for triathletes who want to heal their fear of water yesterday. You may want to know "How long will it take for me to master this calm? How long will it be before I'm ready to again tackle the race that freaked me out, or to do the iron-distance event my heart has been set upon for years?" The answer is:

The slower you go now, the sooner you'll master it.

As great as it would be to give you a timeframe, it can't be done. But if you don't take the time to heal, you will never be safe in deep water, and you will never enjoy your whole triathlon. The method *unequivocally* works if you follow the steps. Here is Maryann, a triathlete who followed the steps and reaped the rewards.

Maryann's Story

"Ten years ago, I decided I wanted to be a triathlete. The only problem was that I couldn't swim. Not only could I not swim. I was terrified in water over my head.

I joined a team and did everything my coach told me to do. When it came to swimming, the instructions were basically to manage my fear, push past it, and suck it up. Everyone else who was afraid seemed to be doing it, so I tried, too. It lasted only so long. I was not having fun. I couldn't understand how I had the endurance to run marathons but could not swim across the pool. I knew there was something else going on.

A few years went by. I searched on the internet for a place where I could find out what was going on so I could stay in the sport of triathlon.

I found something, but it was not convenient, so I put it off. My swimming didn't get better. I finally went to Melon's course. It took me all of the classes to complete the process of learning to swim, which to me meant becoming safe and free in water over my head in a deep pool. The transformation I experienced was beyond words.

I came home and went to my triathlon club's swim practice, and I could do things I'd never been able to do. It was fabulous. I was a new person. My mind had changed so much. I'm still working on being free in open water, and I know I have more to learn. The system of overcoming fear that Melon and Ali are teaching is second to none. Their message is spot on."

It may take days, months, or a couple of years, but healing fear is faster and more gratifying than the alternative—hoping that managing it will make it go away and make you safe. Managing fear will never make you safe. Managed fear always comes back. This is the *catch* about healing fear of water for those who want to be over it yesterday: it takes slowing down. But patience now saves you time, energy, heartache, and maybe your life later on. Our experience is that it can be fully learned in 4-5 weeks of focused practice. However, this practice is so dense that for most people, it takes a year or two. Your inner self as well as your outlook will change!

Like Maryann, you will want to allow yourself the time it takes to become free. The moment you begin to feel frustrated with your progress, you're in the 3rd Circle. Just as food that is cooked in a microwave has its weird uncooked or cold spots, hurrying and feeling anxiety about your path will lead you to an unsatisfactory result. Why not be a crock-pot? Be a Thanksgiving turkey. Take your time and be happy.

Sometimes our students say, "I'm willing to take my time, but how many times per week should I swim while I go through this process?" The answer is the same: whatever it takes to keep you in 1st Circle. Whatever you have time for! Whatever makes you happy! If you schedule three times a week for swimming and it turns out you can only make two of those times, and you get all stressed out about it, is that helpful? Does that take you out of 1st Circle? Would having a once-a-week swim on your calendar make you feel calmer? Once a month? Do whatever works. Do you want to stress yourself out about this? It's about enjoyment, right? Having fun will take you where you want to go.

3.3.2 Taking Time for Self-Care

Self-care means taking care of yourself and honoring how you feel. Committing to staying in the 1st Circle while practicing swimming is an example of excellent self-care. No matter what, whether registering for a triathlon or being in the middle of a race, you can do what is needed to take care of yourself. If that means not signing up for a triathlon until you're ready, give yourself permission to do that. If that means taking the time to clean your goggles so you can see clearly and stay calm, then give yourself permission to do that. It's true that . . .

. . . the time you take will be repaid many times over by the energy and distress you save.

Self-care might seem like a strange thing to you because often in life you've had to "do what you are supposed to do" or "do what you said you would do" or "do what everyone else expects you to do" instead of what you wanted to do. You might have had a duty or expectation to do something even if your body's cues said no. In many situations, pushing past these cues is not dangerous. For example, you might be afraid to give a presentation, but you give it anyway. But in triathlon swimming, you can't safely push the limits of fear—if you do, you put yourself into a dangerous situation that can lead to panic. Avoid panic at all costs.

Self-care in triathlon will help you improve your experience. You will grow as you commit to 1st Circle swimming and doing what is fun.

3.3.3 Getting Past the Past

In your swimming or triathlon life, there have been some not-so-happy places for you in the water where you have been less than in control. Thoughts and ideas of these incidents can be brought to the surface (pun intended) in order to learn from them. Intentional self-observation is the quickest way to progress beyond the effects of a negative history with water. Introspection of this kind can include thinking about how the water makes you feel, as well as what you believe to be true about yourself in the water. As absurd as it might sound, writing a letter to the water and receiving its reply can actually be immeasurably helpful in drawing out your deeply held feelings and beliefs. Get these out on paper so you no longer have to carry them inside you. Start writing, beginning with "Dear Water . . ." Write as much as you want. When you've written all your thoughts and feelings down, write the water's reply. You don't have to share it with anyone. It's just for you.

Are there any other past experiences holding you back? Write about them, too. This is virtually mandatory! Help yourself put the past to rest. You cannot predict what will come of this. It can save you a lot of energy later! When you dump all those feelings onto paper or tell them to someone who can listen neutrally, a shift can happen at the deepest level. Then, remember BE→DO→HAVE. The effects of the shift will ripple out into your swimming.

Once you take that big step, if you do only the things that keep you calm, you are ready to learn to swim.

3.4   Imagine Resting in Water

When was the last time you were still? When you woke up this morning? Besides waking up or falling asleep, how often during the day are you still in both body and mind?

When were you still in the water last? This is the next thing to do when you go swimming. Tell the lifeguard (if there is one) that you're going to practice resting so they're not surprised that you're not moving. Take a breath, settle down in the water on your front, and become still. Find out what happens.

Where do your feet go? Where does your head go? Where do your hands go? Is there any tension? Where is it? Are you doing a lot of work?

Do it again, this time with a bigger breath.
Do it again, this time with a small breath.

See where your feet, head, hand, etc. go, as you did the first time. Were you calm while you did "nothing" there? Did you feel as though you were peacefully in control, which means that you were in the 1st Circle?

You might be thinking "Whoa, this is way too woo-woo for me. All this talk about non-physical part of me and Circles and seeing myself as a whole!?" If this is you, think about how you live and work and exist day to day. Compare it to what this book is saying. In your daily life, your body is here and your mind is there, and it is only when the two work together that you're able to accomplish what you want to do. That is all we're saying. Nothing woo-woo about it.

As you read on, you may feel as though you know the material already. This might be true about some of it, but consider that the reason you have triathlon swim fear is that you may not have the whole story about how your mind and body work together when you're in the water. If you skip over the fundamentals, the whole house comes falling down. Many triathletes have learned this, and they've said things like, "Why didn't anyone tell me this?" and "I never learned this in swim lessons!" and "I never knew this about my body/mind!" The skills in this chapter are the ones most often misunderstood by swim students and triathletes. They are the ones that make you a Swimmer, as opposed to someone who simply performs strokes (see Section 2.2). See if you can find some nuggets here for you. You never know.

Maybe you want the quick answer to what will make this fear thing go away! We understand. Feel the urgency in your body, and allow it to be there! Just sit with it for a while.

More important than advancing quickly is to ensure you aren't skipping steps. You will find that the shortcut to water confidence is taking the time now to learn the basics.

The swimming components described in the next sections begin with the most common skill level we've encountered in triathletes. However, there are more fundamental components and detailed information available in Melon Dash's book *Conquer Your Fear of Water*. If the information presented here seems confusing and seems ahead of where you are, refer to that book as a resource. *Conquer Your Fear of Water* was written as a simple, comprehensive, inexpensive guide to beginning swimming and offers helpful visuals and discussions that underpin the information you find here.

3.4.1 Face in the Water
Just because you've had your face in the water doesn't mean you like it. We have found that many triathletes are not comfortable with it. They force themselves to do it and pretend it doesn't matter. It matters.

They are out of the 1st Circle, and therefore nothing else about swimming is going to work well.

You might be putting your face in with a grimace, visible or not. Similarly, you might be comfortable putting your face in *clear* water, but *not at all* comfortable with murky, dark, or deep water, or water containing vegetation and fish. Knowing your true feelings about having your face in water is an important part of healing fear in triathlon swimming. Trying to swim with your face in the water when you don't want it there causes you to be out of the 1st Circle from the start, and already you are not in control.

If the thought of putting your face into any water—clear, dark, or murky—sounds fine, you can skip this section. But if you're someone who has face-in-the-water issues, it's an important step that cannot be skipped.

What concerns do you have about putting your face in the water? Common concerns include: water in the nose, eyes, mouth, and ears, inhaling water, running out of air, losing balance, losing control or panicking, not being able to come up for air, and claustrophobia. You can take care of every single one of these and feel safe. Remember that we (you and we) don't care if you put your face in at this point. We care only that you feel in control.

Do you know how long you can comfortably have your face in the water? If not, try this experiment. Hold your breath for ten seconds. Is it easy? If so, you might imagine feeling safe putting your face in the water for two seconds. Knowing how long you can hold your breath is handy. Not that we do breath-holding in a triathlon, but while learning to be confident, holding and getting to know your breath is a necessity. To be calm in triathlon swimming, you'll want to become very familiar with your breath, and keeping it comfortable without pushing yourself.

The way to practice the steps below is to do one at a time and to not move forward until you are 100% comfortable (remaining in the 1st Circle) with it. Skipping steps or jumping ahead is *not* more advanced than staying in control. Agreed?

With that agreement, follow these steps to feeling safe putting your face in water.

1. Hold onto the pool wall with one hand.
2. Hold your nose.
3. Take a breath.
4. Close your mouth.
5. Close your eyes.
6. Slowly lower your face close to the water.
7. As you approach the water's surface, and before you reach it, ask yourself if you really want to put your face in. Give yourself permission to say "no" and come back up to rest. When you're ready to approach the water again, take the same steps. Only immerse your face if you're sure you want to. Just dip your face in for a millisecond. You don't need to leave it there. There's no need to put your ears underwater, but you may. Staying in the 1st Circle means you're not pushing yourself at all.
8. Practice this many times. Take breaks as needed.
9. After you're QUITE comfortable with this, when you've had your face in the water for a while, notice your expression under water. Is there any tension? Let it be there. Don't ignore it. If you do, you won't advance.

Here are a few notes that may help you.

- ○ **Remember** the steps you need are included here; you don't have to remember them when you go to the pool. You can get an idea as you read, and then do what your body tells you to do, keeping the book handy in case you want to review. You can also practice many of the skills in a tub that's not too hot (less than 95 degrees Fahrenheit is usually a comfortable temperature for the face).

- ○ **Go slowly.** You'll notice that going slowly is a theme. It gives you the opportunity to be in control—to keep yourself comfortable. Go slowly enough that you are conscious of your choices. Commit yourself to staying in the 1st Circle and not pushing yourself. This is a reliable way to learn.

- ○ **Swallowing water.** If you find you're swallowing while underwater, this is okay. You're not swallowing water, you're simply swallowing. Let it happen; there's no harm in it. Later, when you're more present, it will stop by itself.

If you do find yourself swallowing water, it's not dangerous; it just goes into your stomach. If you're swallowing water because you are out of control, it is being out of control that could lead to danger, not the water intake. (Of course, if you are in water that is not clean, swallowing lots of contaminated water is not safe. If that's a concern to you, you can always ask or look up water safety information for bodies of water and pools or avoid those areas for swimming.) If you're in the ocean, swallowing lots of saltwater can make you nauseous. This is why being in control is so important. When you are in control, it's unlikely swallowing water will happen anymore.

- o **Air in the cheeks.** Often, as someone prepares to go under water, they hold air in their cheeks. This air isn't available to use; it just puffs out your cheeks. The air that you breathe is in your lungs. Your face doesn't have to do any work.

- o **Claustrophobia** in the water is the feeling of being closed in underwater. If this is true of you, know that claustrophobic students have overcome their fear of putting their faces in the water using the steps provided. You can do this, too, if you stay true to yourself. Follow your instinct. If it says, "Don't go in," then don't go in. Just go as far as you feel comfortable, making sure to hold onto the wall and feel safe. Allow yourself to do whatever it takes to stay in the 1st Circle. Give yourself all the time you need. Take breaks and know that claustrophobia will be dismantled if you follow these steps.

When learning the above steps, keep your eyes closed unless it sounds like fun to open them. Water in your eyes makes vision a little blurry, but you can still see. Goggles help keep eyes clear of the chlorine in pools, but they're not absolutely necessary.

3.4.2 Water in the Ears

It's safe to get water in your ears since your ears are like side pockets in your head. Water won't get into your brain, nose, or throat through your ears.

If you're not comfortable putting your ears in water but you'd like to be, follow these steps.

1. Hold onto the wall with one or both hands.
2. Drop down so that your shoulders are under water, if that feels safe.
3. Tip your head sideways, parallel to the surface of the water.
4. As you approach the surface with one earlobe, ask yourself whether you want to put your ear in the water or not. Is there any tension in your body telling you "no"? If so, come up and wait.
5. If not, anticipate the feeling of putting your ear in: the water will feel cool; your hearing will change (sounds will be muffled in that ear); it will fill up with water, which might tickle.
6. Touch your earlobe to the water and see how that feels. If you don't like the idea of submerging your ear, come back up and take a break. The point here is to go slowly and remain present. See if it feels safe.
7. Do this for a while. You decide how slowly and how far to go. When it sounds like fun, you can let a drop of water in, or an earful, if your curiosity takes over. Let the little kid inside you decide.
8. Once you're willing to put your ear in, see how it feels. What does your body do when your ear goes in? Come up as soon as you want to.

Remember that we don't care if you put your ears in the water, we only care that you have fun and remain in control. Once you've become comfortable with submerging one ear, follow the same steps with the other ear. Take your time. Don't push yourself. Remain in the 1st Circle.

On occasion, water doesn't completely drain out of your ears when you come to the surface. Shaking your head usually gets rid of it.

If a gentle shake doesn't do it, then do the following.

1. Move your head quickly in one direction and then stop. The water will keep going.
2. If that doesn't clear your ears, go back under water and fill your ears again. Come back up and try the same thing.
3. If that doesn't clear them, try Swim-Ear or a similar alcohol-based solution from your nearest drugstore. These are made specifically to clear water out of ears.

When you feel okay about putting each of your ears in water, hold the wall and ask yourself if you're ready to try putting your head underwater far enough that both ears go under. If that doesn't sound like fun, feel where the tension appears in your body. Let yourself feel that tension. Don't try to make it disappear; it has a message of protection for you. Take a break if you need to. When you've let tension be, it will start to melt away. This is simply the way it works. If you're in a hurry, you'll delay your learning. If it's not time to put your ears in today, that's fine.

After swimming, allow your ears to dry. If you have long hair, put it behind your ears until your ears air-dry. You would not want to place your head on a pillow and go to sleep when your ear is still wet. You could wake up with Swimmers' Ear, a fungal infection. If you need to dry your ears quickly, remember the saying: "Never put anything smaller than your elbow in your ear." You can hold a hair dryer about an arm's length from your ear, or you can use Swim-Ear as described in step 3 above.

Some swimmers are uncomfortable with the sensation of water becoming "stuck" in their ears during swimming, so they wear earplugs. Just for the record, earplugs themselves can be helpful.

It's a dependence on earplugs for a sense of calm and mindfulness that's isn't helpful. If you realize you could be deriving your sense of safety and calm on earplugs, that could be an issue. For example, if an earplug were to come out during a competition or training swim, how would you feel? Would it take your sense of calm away? Would you like to have calm that transcends having to wear earplugs? You might find that learning how to be comfortable with your ears in the water would make you feel a lot better.

3.4.3 Eyes Without Goggles

Most people want to be able to see in the water. Many have never opened their eyes below the surface. If you wear goggles or a mask, opening your eyes under water is easy, but you may want to know what it's like to do so without goggles so you'll at least be familiar with the feeling. You want to know that if you have your goggles kicked off or fill up in the middle of a race, you won't "lose it."

That said, if putting your eyes into the water and opening them sounds like no fun at all, skip this part for now. Keep them closed or wear goggles. Don't pry your eyes open or force them. Simply let them open when they're ready.

When you put your face into water, notice if there's tension in your eyes. If there is, practice what you're learning: let it be there. Just feel the tension. Don't tell yourself to relax. Don't force your eyes open. When you have allowed tension to be there, what do you think will happen?

The tension in your eyes starts to disappear, or your eyes open. If not, feel and allow the tension again. You'll notice it requires just the slightest bit of tension to keep your eyes closed. If you allow that tension, what happens? Your eyes open on their own. You can see. It will be blurry, but you can see.

How does it feel on your eyeballs to open your eyes? Only open them as much as you want to; it doesn't hurt. The view is blurry because there's no air space in front of your eyes. If you were to leave your eyes open for 5-10 minutes in most chlorinated pools, they might burn a bit from the chemical balance. This doesn't cause damage, but it can be uncomfortable. This is why so many people use goggles. They provide good vision and comfort for the eyes.

It's good to spend time in the pool every day with your face in the water and your eyes open so it becomes natural and comfortable. After it becomes second nature to open your eyes under water, you may want to go back to goggles. It's fine to spend all your time in the water without goggles, but seeing well gives you more control.

If you wear glasses and can't see well without them, and if taking them off makes you uncomfortable in the water, you have several options:

o Wear them in the pool or lake. This works while you're above the surface, of course. Use a retaining strap to avoid losing them.
o Wear contact lenses under goggles.
o Purchase goggles that have your prescription ground into the lenses.

3.4.4 Your Eyes with Goggles

The main advantage of goggles is that you can see clearly under water. There are hundreds of models of goggles on the market, and they fit all kinds of faces. A great pair for one person could be unworkable for another. Find a pair that fits your face comfortably and doesn't leak.

To find goggles, go to a swimming supply or sporting goods store and ask if they have unpackaged goggles you can try on. If not, they may let you open packages.

Put the goggles against your face without the strap around your head, then press them into your eye sockets and see if they create suction. If they do, they are likely to fit you. If they are the type that doesn't rely on suction, it will say so on the package; follow the instructions for fitting. Most goggles are the suction type.

If you want vision correction in your goggles, there are inexpensive models ground to a certain diopter. You can buy them over the counter at many swimming gear and sporting goods stores. Some optometrists grind goggles to match your exact prescription. Check to see which models can be ground, then choose one that fits your face.

There are also several types of masks that are larger and more comfortable than goggles for some people and that don't cover the nose. Ask to try on a swimmer's mask such as the AquaSphere brand. You can't be sure until you get into the pool if a pair will be leak-proof, so be sure to ask the store about their return policy.

Once you begin to wear goggles, occasionally remove them and practice opening your eyes under water without them. This helps you to practice control without goggles. You want to know that you can remain in control if you ever find yourself in the water without them.

3.4.5 Letting Go of the Nose

When you put your face and ears in the water earlier, you either held your nose or you didn't. If you'd like to keep your nose sealed, you can either hold your nose or use a nose clip. If you hold it, you occupy that hand. You can learn to keep water out of your nose without using a clip or your hand.

Holding your nose, put your face in the water as you have been doing it. Once there, while you're feeling completely in control—and if it sounds like fun—add one new thing: release your grip on your nose, keeping your hand in the same spot. Don't change anything but that one small thing: letting go of your nose. You won't get water in your nose. You won't inhale because you're present, you're still, and you're doing only one thing.

When you take your fingers off your nose under water, your nostrils fill with water. This is not the same as "getting water up your nose," which is when water goes into your sinus cavities. Having your nostrils fill with water is possibly a new sensation, and for some people it takes a few minutes of practice for several days to get used to it. When water takes up the space in your nostrils, it fills them just as it would fill an empty glass if you placed it in the water. See if the sensation is okay with you. Get accustomed to this new feeling. Hold your nose again if you want to take a break from the feeling. Soon, you'll find it's safe to have your nose unplugged in the water.

A nose clip also frees your hands and therefore gives you more control. Many people think of it as a crutch. Others consider it "cheating." In truth, it's neither a crutch nor cheating. It helps you to be in your body. Why not make it easy for yourself? A nose clip is a stepping stone. You'll stop using it when you can be present with your nose open.

A nose clip can be anything from a clothespin to a $15 colored designer item. Nose clips usually cost $3-5. Different brands have different shapes, and certain ones will fit your nose better than others. Nose clips will fall off if you have sunblock or moisturizer on your nose. You may have to invest a few dollars and use trial and error to find the best one for you.

When selecting a nose clip, test it to make sure it stays on your face and no water enters your nose. Found a good one? Buy two. If you're thinking you don't want to use a nose clip because in the long run you don't want to wear one, please reconsider. Today is not the long run. Today is "comfort priority day." Do what will make you most comfortable today. What you want for the long run will take care of itself. Being in the 1st Circle is your first priority.

If you don't want to depend on a clip for your safety in a race, good thinking! But we are not at race time yet. We are at learning time, and to learn you need to feel safe. Feeling safe about your nose allows you to focus on other things. Focusing on your nose will lead to freedom from a nose clip. Focusing on other things may require that your nose's safety comes from wearing a clip. You will evolve past the nose clip if you allow yourself to use it until it feels like time to take the next step.

Be kind to yourself. There's no hurry. Practice having your face under water with your fingers a millimeter from your nose. You know that you won't inhale because you're in control. Feel what it's like to have your nose open. Practice this thirty times or one hundred times, and take your time.

When you become comfortable having your nose free, you'll be able to move your hand away from your face and know that your nose is safe. Your nose is safe because you know what you're doing: you're there.

The sensation of "getting water up your nose" is actually getting water in your sinuses. The bones and cartilage around your nose form a circle at the top of your nose, and your sinuses are beyond it. If water goes beyond this circle, it enters your sinuses. We want to avoid this whenever possible because it's quite uncomfortable. You wouldn't want to become accustomed to the discomfort of getting water in your sinuses because: 1) if you're uncomfortable, you're a step closer to the 5th Circle; 2) too much water in the nose (sinuses) can cause a sinus infection; and 3) water in your sinuses isn't fun.

As long as your head doesn't tip backward or upside down (and if you don't inhale through your nose when it's under water), the water in your nostrils will not get into your sinuses. If your face is aimed straight down or straight ahead in the water, all the water in your nostrils will stay in your nostrils and cause no discomfort. If your head is in an upright position, you will not get water into your sinuses (your "nose") unless, of course, you inhale—in other words, if you're not in 1st Circle.

However, if you . . .
   o Turn upside down,
   o Do a somersault,
   o Look upward while under water, or
   o Put your head backward too far while you're in a back float,

. . . the water in your nostrils will go into your sinuses unless you know how to prevent it. You'll probably come up and sneeze.

You can prevent from getting water in your nose by:

- o Not moving your nose through the water like a scoop.
- o Using a nose clip.
- o Holding your nose.
- o Exhaling through your nose anytime your head is in any compromised position. It's completely safe and comfortable to be upside down or turning somersaults in the water. You won't get water in your nose if, as you turn, you exhale through your nose the whole time. The air coming out of your nose will prevent water from coming in. It must be exhaled 100% of the time your nose is in a compromised position. Exhaling through your mouth will not keep water out of your nose.

"Blipping" is an abbreviated version of exhaling through your nose in the water. To blip, inhale through your mouth above the surface, then exhale a bubble or two of air through your nose the moment you put your face in the water. Stop exhaling after your nose is below the surface. Just a few bubbles of "blipping" outward prevent you from getting water in your nose. If you don't blip, you may not get water into your nose, either . . . but if you want to ensure no water, blip.

Give yourself lots of time to become comfortable with blipping. Make it a habit. The habit of blipping to keep water out of your nose is worth every minute you put into it. Give yourself enough time to practice and embody it—or give yourself permission to use a nose clip.

Use the nose clip in shallow open water when you practice. But before you race, take time to slow down and practice the new skill of being able to swim without it in training so you won't need it when you race. As you know, you wouldn't want your safety in a race to depend on your nose clip. It has to come from yourself.

Once you can have your hands free of your nose and you're at ease with your face in the water, you will have reached a milestone. Don't try to move on until you're happy having your face and ears in the water. Keep your nose and ears happy at all times.

3.5   Stillness in the Water

Many times we think of swimming as active motion. However, did you know that much of swimming is underpinned by stillness rather than movement? Your arms and legs can be moving; your mind can be still.

3.5.1   Do You Float, or Do You Sink?

This section contains information you may or may not have learned in swim lessons. Instead of rushing through this, review it carefully. Most often, this is the stuff people say they were never taught.

You may have seen the meme that's made the rounds on social media. It says, "In the bike portion of the triathlon, if you stop moving, you just fall over. In the run, if you stop moving, you just sit down. But in the swim, if you stop moving, you drown!"

This is damaging misinformation.

If you stop moving, you will likely float. However, if you're very lean *and* you expel too much air (which you would only do if you don't know how water works), you'll sink. If you don't know "deep down" how the water and your body work together, it's not time yet for you to attempt a triathlon.

Most people can float with little to no effort. Sinking, on the other hand, requires effort for most people.

Let's figure out what kind of body you have in the world of buoyancy. There are two kinds of people: floaters and sinkers (non-floaters).

Floaters
A floater is someone whose body is naturally buoyant with air in his or her lungs, and usually even without holding air in the lungs. Floaters don't have to do anything to keep their faces above water in a back float. In a front float, the back of their heads remain above the surface, and their feet may hang down and touch the floor in shallow water—but the person remains floating (Figure 3.5.1a). Are you a floater or a sinker?

Figure 3.5.1a. Many good floating positions.

The amount of air floaters have at any given moment affects their buoyancy. The bigger the breath, the higher the float. The adipose tissue (fat) they have also affects how buoyant they are. The more fat there is, the higher the float. This is one instance where it's handy if you haven't lost that extra 15 pounds. It's perfectly safe to be lean, too.

Buoyancy not only keeps floaters at the surface, but it also brings them back to the top from depth if they jump in. Consider someone jumping into the deep end of a pool. Gravity takes them down into the water, and their buoyancy brings them back up. If you take a good breath before you jump and you hold it, you'll be more buoyant and will rise sooner and faster than if you take a small breath. Not that you need to hurry.

When you jump in, your head may go three or four feet below the surface, depending on how far above the surface you are when you jump and how streamlined you are as you enter. The further up you start, the deeper you go. The more streamlined you are when you enter (vertical, arms and legs together), the deeper you go. In the past, when you jumped in you may have swum back to the surface. But have you ever tried jumping in while holding your breath and then not doing anything at all? Not a darn thing?

If you're a floater and you're comfortable doing this with a lifeguard or instructor in the water with you, try this: jump off the side, take a big breath, hold your nose, and just wait. See how you float back to the surface with no effort.

Pushing off the bottom—if you descend that far—or swimming up with an arm sweep or two will bring a sinker to the surface. Of course, swimming up brings everyone back to the top, but for floaters, remaining still and floating back to the surface teaches you how little work is necessary. It takes just a few seconds longer for the water to push you back up than it does to swim up, depending on how deep you go. Most pools aren't more than twelve feet deep, which is deep enough that you probably won't reach the bottom by jumping off the side. Floaters float up because buoyancy (air and fat) overcomes gravity. The point is that floaters will float up no matter what they do unless they purposely stay down.

Remember: the most important part is being in control. Stay with your body, wherever it is in the water column. If your feet are near the bottom, don't let your attention be at the top. Stay with your body. This is the mindfulness that overcomes panic.

Will floaters float to the surface if they have expelled all their air? Maybe, and maybe not. It depends on whether or not they lose their buoyancy when they expel air. You can only know this by testing it. To test it, try sitting on the bottom of the pool in shallow water and staying there for four or five seconds with your suit touching the bottom (Figures 3.5.1b and 3.5.1c). If you're able to sit, you've found roughly how much air you must expel to lose your buoyancy. If you sit for a moment and start to float back up, you didn't lose your buoyancy. Some people have enough fat that even if they expel all the air they possibly can, they will still be buoyant. Remember, it's impossible to expel *all* your air. Your body retains a residual volume of air in your lungs that prevents your lungs from collapsing even when you've expelled all the air you can. It doesn't take much fat to be *unable* to sink.

Figure 3.5.1b. Happy on the bottom.

If you don't expel any air and you sink to the bottom, you're a sinker. This is a testament to your fitness because you must have lots of muscle and very little fat for this to happen. It's not bad, unfortunate, or annoying to be a sinker . . . unless you think so! It's okay. You have other things going for you.

Once you have expelled all the air you can, your body's fat stores will determine how you float. Try it out and see how the water works with your body. Eventually, after trying to sit on the bottom and coming up to the surface a number of times, you will feel your body's buoyancy and how it works. Do this until you're convinced of your buoyancy. You must be unequivocally certain.

Figure 3.5.1c. Relaxing on the bottom.

Sinkers

A sinker is someone who sinks to the bottom when they fill their lungs with air and lie on the water (Figures 3.5.1b and 3.5.1c). Sinkers are rare individuals who typically have extremely low body fat, such as Olympic athletes and pro triathletes. These people need to move a bit in order to remain at the water's surface but can still remain in control peacefully if they know what they're doing. They can easily get air when they want it and can stay at the surface. There is absolutely no reason to leave the 1st Circle if you're a sinker once you've learned how it all works. To be safe, learn this and be certain. The information you need is here. Take it to the water.

A combination of different positions can be used by floaters or sinkers to rest in water of any depth to get air using very little effort. The three main positions are the front float, back float, and vertical float. You may find the below descriptions useful. Even if you think you already know them, check again.

3.5.2   On the Front

Assuming you've learned to be comfortable putting your face in water, go to water that's about chest level. Then, hold onto the side of the pool with both hands, your feet on the floor. Take a breath and lower your face and body into the water as far as the water allows. Let the water to the work. Your hands will be holding the edge and will prevent you from drifting away.

Do you feel the water holding you up, or are your hands or feet holding you up? Take the pressure off your hands if there is any (keeping them on the edge) and see what the water does for you. Do this enough times that you can find a position at the wall that feels like you've been shot by an elephant tranquilizer dart. Holding muscle tension takes energy, and tension signifies worry. We must remove all reasons for worry.

If you're a floater, you'll feel the water holding you up. Spend some time feeling this, coming up for air as needed. Allow your feet to remain on the floor if they don't float up on their own. If your legs are muscular, they are denser than water and your feet will rest on the bottom. This is normal. Some people float vertically, others diagonally, and others horizontally.

Notice that it's the water holding you up, not your hands or feet. True?

"But if my feet are on the floor, how can I be floating?"

You are floating with your feet on the floor! How do you know you're floating? Imagine where you would go if the water were suddenly removed. If you would fall to the bottom, the water is holding you up; you're floating. Don't worry. Almost everyone thinks a proper float is a horizontal one, or at least one with their feet off the floor in shallow water. This is one of the misunderstandings that has prevented millions from learning to swim.

If your feet float up, it's natural. Allow it. But don't lift your feet off the floor. Find your most effortless position while holding onto the edge.

We're not suggesting you take your hands off the edge and hold them in the air. That will make you sink an inch or so since your hands can't float in the air. The weight of your hands above the water pushes you downward a bit. Just let them rest on the edge of the pool.

If you're not a floater, you'll feel your knees sink, and you'll probably find yourself in a kneeling position on the floor of the pool. Are you in your body there (in complete control)? If so, you're on track. Try again, and take more air this time. A bigger breath can be the difference between floating and sinking. Get to know your air. If you sink back to the bottom after taking your biggest breath, you're a sinker. This is not a bad thing! In fact, it's a very good thing to know.

After practicing feeling the water hold you up, you may let go of the wall, *but only if you can remain calm*. If you can't remain in control, do not—we repeat, do not—attempt it. Losing control is an injury you must prevent. Remember, you're learning to *heal* fear, not to manage it, and certainly not to prolong it or decrease your self-trust. You'll be able to stay calm (in the 1st Circle) if you know how to stand up from a front float ("unfloat"), either by holding onto the edge or standing up from a front float. If you're not sure you can stand up in control, go to shallower water, or ask someone to stand next to you to help you up if you feel rushed inside. We insist that you not cut corners on this because you won't get what is available, which is essential! This is non-negotiable!

Wherever there is tension, take a minute to recognize it and allow it to be there. Don't hurry it away. By fully allowing tension to be there, you become fully present to it for the first time. You don't want to fight this. **This is healing!** When you allow it to be there, you're giving it an opportunity to disappear, and it will . . . unless you're looking for it to disappear. That's not the 1st Circle. Slow down and be in the moment with your body. If you are too afraid, go back a step to something that's completely comfortable. That may mean floating while holding onto the wall, with no intention of letting go of the wall. Camp there quietly for a while. It may mean learning in a two-foot pool. Let yourself do it. You have to feel 100% safe in order to learn and have it stick. More on "unfloating" later.

Remember, doing a front float doesn't mean having to float horizontally at the surface. The front float takes on its own angle of repose depending on your air supply and body density, and may show all sorts of interesting angles from one person to the next (see Figure 3.5.1a). Don't spend time and energy trying to float horizontally if your body doesn't naturally float in this position. All you need to do is let the water do all the work. Let your float be where it is, and just rest there. Sometimes it's hard to let yourself be tense; you want to change it. But if you allow it, it has its first chance to evolve organically into something else. Be in the 1st Circle. Are you learning what that means? Do you know what it feels like?

Another float similar to the front float is the prone float. This can be described as holding your arms and legs up in a "Superman pose." The prone float takes a bit more effort and is not used for resting. It's a building block for learning strokes. We'll talk more about the prone float further in the book when we address freestyle. For now, it's too much information.

3.5.3 On Your Back

Being on one's back in the water is often misunderstood. Many triathletes believe they can't be on their backs because they'll sink. This may be due to the belief that a correct back float is performed horizontally. Do you find your abdominal muscles engaging during your back float, trying to lift your legs up? If so, you could find yourself with your face under water. This isn't very helpful for breathing, is it? How is it supposed to work? Feel the tension in your abs while you float and let it be there. If you do, your legs will likely fall to where they should be. Having your nose and mouth out of the water is the important thing, not having your legs up.

Two-Foot Pool
The best place to learn a back float is in a two-foot-deep or "beach-entry" (or "zero depth") pool where you can put your hands on the bottom (Figure 3.5.3a). This is an easy place to determine whether you're a floater or a sinker.

Figure 3.5.3a. Back floating in a two-foot pool. (Photo by Melon Dash)

The first few times you do this, it's best to use a nose clip in the event your face goes under water. If you can find such a pool, sit on the bottom with your hands beside you.

Lower your head and ears back into the water, keeping your hands on the bottom. Let yourself down into the water far enough that it can hold you. Let your heels stay on the bottom; don't lift them. If they float up, fine. If they stay down, fine.

See if you can feel the water holding you up, or if your hands are holding you up. Keeping your hands on the bottom, experiment with taking a big breath and holding it as you lie back on the water. What happens?

If you sink while holding the biggest possible breath, then as we said above, you're a sinker and you'll need to learn to "scull" to keep your nose and mouth out of water. For now, make sure you don't sink on account of trying to lift your feet off the floor! If you lift your feet, your face will likely go under.

If you float without holding your breath, or while holding a medium-sized breath, you are a floater. Get to know what floating feels like. You want to know in your bones that the water holds you up.

While floating, what happens if you exhale a bit? A lot? Spend time playing with this. You want to be very familiar with your air and how it affects your buoyancy. Find a comfortable balance between inhaling and exhaling and staying afloat. You're finding your natural, effortless float.

If You Don't Have a Two-Foot Pool

If you don't have access to a two-foot pool, face the wall in chest-deep water and hold onto it with both hands, promising yourself you won't let go. Press your body flush against the wall with the tops of your feet on the floor. Lower yourself so that your shoulders are under water, and slowly lean back into the water, putting your ears in. Let your head rest in the water as though it were on your pillow. Don't support yourself with your feet. See if you can feel the water holding you (Figure 3.5.3b).

Experiment with taking the biggest possible breath and holding it as you lie back on the water. What happens?

This is a good test to do while wearing a nose clip. Otherwise, if you dip below the surface, you'll get water in your nose. As we said above, if you sink even while holding a huge breath, you're a sinker. It's okay to be a sinker!

Figure 3.5.3b. Letting the water hold her up at the wall.

If you float, hold a comfortable breath next time and see how floating feels. Practice this many, many times. Next, lie back without holding your breath and see how well you float. Get to know what floating feels like. You want to know in your bones that the water holds you up; you are a floater.

While floating, what happens if you exhale a bit? A lot? Spend time playing with this. You want to be very familiar with your air and how it affects your buoyancy. As you play with exhaling, you'll notice it causes your face to lower closer to the surface. Exhaling and inhaling are your control mechanisms for keeping your nose above water. There are other mechanisms, but this is the first you should learn.

Find the balance between inhalation and exhalation that keeps you comfortable. What amount of air in your lungs keeps your nose, mouth, and chin above the surface without strain? What amount of air allows your breathing to be easy? Figuring this out, you're on your way to a natural, effortless float. Experiment with this until it's reliable and comfortable.

If you take a big breath and hold it, your face will be as high above the surface as it can be. Holding your breath isn't sustainable, but it does teach you how high above the surface you're capable of floating.

Unfloating

The next step is to teach yourself to unfloat: to stand up from the float.

When you want to stop floating at the wall, you tip your head forward and contract your abs to stand up. You may be using your hands a bit, too. Now repeat this many times (25? 50?) and notice how you stand up. Do the work with your abs and neck and lessen the role of your hands. Do your legs come into play?

You'll use the same actions if you are floating away from the wall. You'll add one thing: drawing your knees toward your head. So it will feel like this: You're floating on your back away from the wall. You become *fully present* to the back float, feeling the water hold you up, allowing your feet to go where they naturally go, and resting. *You're not planning ahead for the unfloat!*

When you want to unfloat, contract your abs, tip your head forward, take a breath, and draw your knees toward your head. Your body will move into a ball and start to slowly rotate forward by itself. Your face will go into the water. When your balance feels "just so"—and you'll know that when you get to it—you can place your feet on the bottom. It requires virtually no effort.

If you don't feel capable of remaining in control when you do this, ask someone to spot you, or learn it in shallower water or in a two-foot pool. You can also wait until later to learn it.

Other Ways to Back Float
You can make your face float higher in the water if you want to. A mechanism to keep your face above the surface without extra movement is to float in the shape of an I, T, or Y (Figures 3.5.3c, 3.5.3d, and 3.5.3e). Before trying this, you must be comfortable without holding your breath on your back. Don't try it until you are comfortable, or you'll scare yourself.

Float on your back with your arms in the position they naturally take, which may be the "I" position (Figure 3.5.3c). Keeping your arms *below the surface*, move them slowly toward your head so that your torso and arms form a T (Figure 3.5.3d). This moves your center of buoyancy toward your head, allowing you to become more horizontal, which will lift your face higher. Moving your arms beyond your head into a Y-shaped position with your arms at 10 o'clock and 2 o'clock may allow you to float even higher (Figure 3.5.3e).

Clockwise from top left: "I" position (Figure 3.5.3c), "T" position (Figure 3.5.3d), and "Y" position (Figure 3.5.3e) floats.

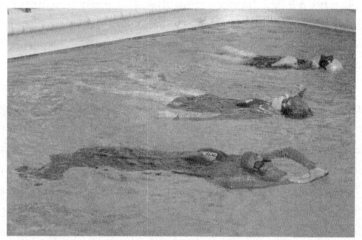

Figure 3.5.3f. Back float positions.
Bottom student: With her hands beyond her head, her lower half rises, making it easy to keep her face out. This is similar to the "Y" position (Figure 3.5.3e). The other two women are more buoyant.

At any time while on your back, your feet may drop partway or all the way to the bottom (in shallow water) and you may think you're floating incorrectly. You're not! Keep reminding yourself: floating on your back does not have to be horizontal. The important thing is that your face is out of the water. Recall that the two enablers of floating—air and fat—are mostly located in the chest and torso. These make the top half of your body float quite nicely if you are a floater. However, the lower half does not typically have large quantities of air (unless you have some kind of air-filled leg bone implant!). Therefore, attempting to lift your legs backfires, and as you struggle to keep your feet up, your face goes under.

V-Float

If you do try to lift your legs or feet, your body will reach a position like the letter V. This either pulls your face underwater or throws you off balance. To avoid this, feel the tension you're holding in your abs. This tension is in the way, as is your belief that you should hold your legs up. Let your legs fall wherever they naturally fall. Your upper body will remain floating. Your feet will fall to where they should be.

You may be thinking, "But if I let my legs start to sink, won't they continue sinking and take me to the bottom?" Interestingly, the answer is no—unless you're a sinker. For floaters, your relaxed legs will continue sinking *only* to a point at which your float comes to the signature angle that is right for you, and there you will reach a happy little floating equilibrium with your face out of the water and your legs dangling down like a jellyfish (See Figures 3.5.3g, h, i, and j). The great thing about this position on your back is that you can remain at rest as long as you like—you could be fed bits of cheeseburger and sports drink and stay in the water until you turn into a prune.

Sinking Below the Surface

If it feels as though your face is about to go under water, pushing down on the water with your hands will lift your face up. If somehow you do submerge, breathing out through your nose as you go under will prevent water from getting in. Exhaling air through your nose makes it impossible for water to come in. Stay in the 1st Circle as you experiment. Remember: *it is more advanced to stay calm than it is to do the skill and lose your calm.* If exhaling through your nose makes you leave the 1st Circle, go back a step to floating while holding your breath.

Sculling

If you're a sinker, or if you have trouble tipping your head back in a back float, you can keep your face above water by sculling: moving your arms and hands in a way that creates lift. As you practice this, consider wearing a nose clip to keep your nose happy. Here are some ideas:

- o   Sculling. Angle your hands at 30 degrees to the surface while sweeping gently back and forth, pressing on the water with your palms and turning your palms as they reach the end of each sweep (Figures 3.5.3g and 3.5.3h, i, and j). Your palms are *always* flat to get lift or propulsion from your upper body in swimming. If you find this motion hard to picture, try going online and searching "sculling in swimming" for some short online videos.
- o   Some people like to use a gentle downward motion with both hands to create lift.

Figures 3.5.3g and h. Sculling motions. This man is lean yet is able to keep his face above water by moving his hands efficiently. This is called sculling. Sculling is sweeping the hands and arms back and forth just below the surface, hands pitched. The photos above show the outsweep; the photos below show both the outsweep and the insweep. Above, at the 3 o'clock and 9 o'clock positions, he will turn his hands and sweep back to 6 o'clock.

Outsweep   Insweep

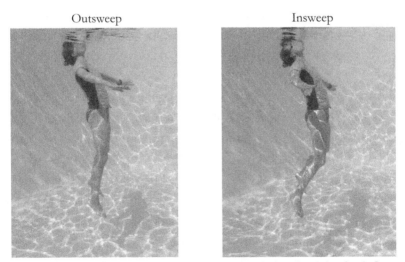

Figures 3.5.3i and j. Outsweep and insweep of sculling. This is her back float. She's a sinker, so she needs to get lift from her hands (or legs) to keep her face out of the water.

What feels best to you?

For floaters and sinkers alike, if keeping water out of your nose remains a problem while playing with and learning the back float, use a nose clip. Though the words "nose clip" may recall hot days at summer camp with canoes and stretched-out swimsuits, know that some incredibly cool Olympic swimmers use them in backstroke races. We urge you to use one as a stepping stone as you learn if it helps you enjoy your swimming and stay in your body. Let no one give you a hard time. You are cool with us.

3.5.4 Vertical Position

Why be vertical? If you go to the pool during a session for anything other than lap swimming, most of the people in the water will be vertical. If you go under water to keep an eye on your kids, or to watch an underwater demonstration, you will be vertical. Being comfortable vertically in deep water is a requirement of knowing how to swim. It's one of the ways we can come to a full stop and rest. It doesn't require having your head above water.

This involves balance. Floaters can float like a weightless astronaut in a space shuttle. Sinkers can scull to remain at the surface. In this position, your body is positioned straight up and down with the top of your head at the surface of the water. It is similar to the front float because you can't breathe, but you can still rest away from any commotion at the surface without worrying about choking on water. It's important to be comfortable being vertical in the water, whether your head is in or out. In the pool, it can be a very fun float to play with. See how bending your legs or arching your torso one way or the other causes a vertical float to slowly become either a front float or a back float.

3.5.5 A Note About Treading Water

If you know about treading water, you may be wondering, "How is vertical floating different from treading water? Aren't they both vertical?" The answer is yes—but treading water means keeping your head completely out of the water all the time as you remain in one place, vertically.

Treading is performed by moving the hands back and forth at a pitched angle, or paddling, or kicking, or all of that at once. Treading water is essentially swimming in place. It's a convenience skill, not a safety skill. It's one of the more advanced skills to master, as the weight of the head (roughly 11 pounds) has to be overcome by the treading movement. Imagine holding a very fat dachshund over your head and trying to stay at the surface. That's what you're trying to do when you tread. No wonder it's more difficult to learn than most swimming skills. The good news is that treading isn't necessary to be a Swimmer. We know you want to learn it, and it will come to you once you've mastered the water.

Treading can be useful when you need to talk, look around, or have uninterrupted eye contact with a buoy, boat, or person for a few moments. But hear us, dear pilgrim, it is *not* essential to swimming or being calm in deep water! It is just not. There are other easier ways to have your face above water to breathe or communicate.

Before you move on to the next section, spend time absorbing these floats and positions. Take time to physically and mentally embody each one and understand it. Repeat them all until you've mastered them. If you're unsure, that means you haven't mastered them yet! Until you do, it won't be time to move on to the next step.

3.6   Control in the Water

As you move in the water, keep yourself happy. Maintain the commitment to stay in the 1st Circle. The choreography of *how* you move forward is not the point. Feeling safe is the point.

Have you ever swum freestyle in the 3rd Circle? Have you ever been in a front float pulling yourself forward while in the 3rd Circle? Not taking care of yourself in the 1st Circle results in a host of outcomes to be avoided at all costs: experiencing the fear of sinking, panicking, being kicked and jostled, not being able to rest, being left alone or behind, getting too tired, not being able to finish the swim, getting water in your nose, swallowing water and not being able to regroup, coughing, feeling sick, or wanting to give up. Save yourself all that pain by staying in the 1st Circle. If that means not swimming, fine. If it means going slower than molasses, swimming apart from the crowd, swimming on your back, or resting on a surfboard—fine.

You can give yourself permission to have these concerns and learn how to take care of them one by one as you practice the skills in this section, **committing to only doing the ones you can stay in the 1st Circle for,** and progressing through the skills only as you learn to be in complete control. Remember, we (you and we) do not care whether you do a skill. We care that you stay comfortable and safe. First, learn to stay safe. The fancier things come later. If you don't build a foundation of safety now, you won't have those two legs to stand on later (presence of mind and understanding how the water works). We know pushing yourself in this situation is counterproductive. Rest assured that sticking with this process WILL get you where you want to go the soonest it can be done.

3.6.1 Propelling on Your Front

Let's imagine someone is standing in four feet of water and is given the task of retrieving a rubber ducky floating 20 feet away. Given enough time, she would probably figure out how to sweep her hands through the water as she walked toward the ducky. She would produce movement intuitively since she felt safe with the bottom beneath her. She can do this without being taught because when she's calm and able to receive feedback from her surroundings, she intuitively allows what she knows about forward movement on land to translate to the water.

This is to say that when you push backward on any water, deep or shallow, your body moves forward (Figure 3.6.1a). This is true no matter what position you float in. Visualize pushing backward on the water and moving forward. Can you "feel" the resistance when you push back on the dense medium of water?

To create forward propulsion on your front, start in a front float. Sweep both arms backward at the same time, pushing on the water with your flat palms and the inner surface of your arms. After sweeping your arms backward to your thighs, draw your hands close under your belly and extend them forward so that you're stretched out like Superman, looking downward. Your legs will trail behind you, which will cause a bit of drag. But as mentioned previously, you'll still be able to make progress without fatiguing. Most likely you can propel yourself this way already. But can you breathe? Learn to get air in the sections on bobbing and breathing. Make sure you can envision yourself swimming the whole tri swim this way, or rolling onto your back. It's reliable . . . so it's a winner.

Figures 3.6.1a, 3.6.1b, and 3.6.1c, clockwise from top left. In the top left photo, she begins her pull with both arms at 12 o'clock. She sweeps backward to her thighs with straight arms, pushing on the water with the inside of her arms and her flat palms. You can see her legs are moving, however they're not needed; the arms can do all the work by themselves while the legs trail behind. She is looking forward rather than down.

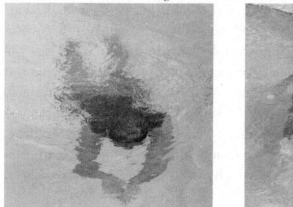

Figures 3.6.1d and 3.6.1e. Propelling on the front with both arms, legs trailing behind.

Do this for the distance that's comfortable for your breath. Do it many, many times! Get very comfortable with it. Notice if there's any tension. As long as there's tension, there's a belief that you're not safe. Back up to a simpler step and make it safe for yourself before practicing any longer. Yes, you will be limited by not being able to get a new breath. That's okay for now. You're learning propulsion, not breathing.

With all of this chitchat about mechanics, you may be wondering when we're going to show you how to swim really fast. The answer is we're not—the topic of how to swim fast is outside the scope of this book. Mechanics are indeed important if swimming fast is eventually your goal, but not as important as having the real Swimming basics: peace of mind.

3.6.2 Propelling on Your Back

Propelling yourself on your back is very similar to propelling on your front. Start with a comfortable, safe back float. Then propel yourself using three simple movements to push the water backward toward your feet. These motions, individually labeled for kids, are the "monkey," the "airplane," and the "pencil." They create forward momentum by drawing the hands up to the underarms like a monkey, extending them out to the sides like an airplane, and sweeping them forward to align with the body like a pencil (Figure 3.6.2).

Monkey   Airplane   Pencil

Figure 3.6.2 Propelling on the back.

3.6.3 Bobbing

It is possible while you're in a vertical position to apply downward pressure on the water with your arms in order to bounce up to get air. This action is commonly known as bobbing, because the top of the head looks like an apple bobbing at a Halloween party (Figures 3.6.3a and 3.6.3b).

Start by standing in four or five feet of water. With a good breath, bend your knees until your face goes below the water's surface, exhaling though your nose as you go under. Exhale until you're ready for more air. Then stand up to inhale. Do this a hundred times. Take your time. Make it easy for yourself. Get the feeling of a comfortable exchange of air. If your air doesn't flow freely, let it come out in fits and starts, and notice how it stops. As you notice it and allow it, it will begin to smooth out.

After it's comfortable to bob with your feet on the bottom, float vertically in the shallow end with your knees bent so your feet are off the floor, behind you. In bobbing, you exhale a tiny bit of air through your nose to keep water out as gravity pulls you down a few inches. Then gravity loses its pull and buoyancy takes over. As buoyancy takes over, on your way up, press your arms/hands downward, exhaling your air. Your head bobs up above the surface as you exhale the last of a comfortable exhalation. You'll have plenty of time to take a nice, refreshing breath before gravity gently pulls you back down into the water. Gravity then gives up and buoyancy takes over.

Figures 3.6.3a and 3.6.3b. Various stages of bobbing.

On your ascent, expel your air so that as you rise above the surface, your lungs are empty enough to be ready to receive a new breath. You wouldn't want to stack a new breath on top of an old one; that would make you winded.

If you exhale too much air on the descent, you might expel your buoyancy. Exhale a few bubbles of air to keep water out of your nose on the descent, but keep most of your air in your lungs for exhalation on the way back up. The air in your lungs and any other buoyancy you have stop your descent and start your ascent. After your ascent has begun, pushing downward with your arms accelerates it (not that you would be in a hurry) and guarantees you'll come back up through the surface. Don't try to exhale *and* inhale during the brief time you're up. It's exhausting.

The inhalation should not be a huge gulp of air but a comfortable, walking-down-the-street-sized inhalation.

Press downward on the water enough to lift yourself just above the surface (chin comes out). If you push down too hard, you'll come up too high—and as great as Newton's equal and opposite reaction law is, the law also bites back by causing you to go deep (a foot or so) below the surface after coming up too far. Doing this can be energy consuming. It might be fun to experiment with doing as little work as possible to bob your mouth above the water to get a comfortable breath, and then allow yourself to drop under again.

When you're under water, you can hang out there and rest if you wish, as long as your air allows. Then bob as needed.

If you're practicing bobs and find yourself feeling out of breath or lightheaded, your air exchange is uneven. You're probably inhaling more than you're exhaling. Could this be because you are starting while you're tense and out of the 1st Circle? If yes, slow down. Don't rush. Proceed calmly. Go back to standing and practicing bobbing. Once you truly have mastered that, then, hold onto the wall in five or six feet of water and push up on the wall to take yourself under. Then come back up, focusing on breathing comfortably. Once you are breathing comfortably, try bobbing without holding the wall.

You will want to learn this in the safety of a pool because if you feel out of breath, you will likely leave the 1st Circle. No one needs to tell you that it's hard to stay calm when you're out of air and you aren't certain of your safety. When you're calm, bobbing is a very slow and peaceful activity. It can be done almost indefinitely and is a useful open-water skill.

3.6.4 Breathing: Horizontal Bobbing Equals "Pop-Up" Breaths

Another way to get air is to swim calmly on your front, sweeping with both arms at the same time from front to back.

When you're ready to take a breath, press outward and downward with your arms. This brings your head above water long enough for a breath. Use your neck to bring your head up, too. Exhale at the same time you press outward to expel air prior to popping up above the water (Figure 3.6.4).

If you're calm when you do this, you'll feel that expelling air empties your lungs, allowing you to get a breath when you come up. This is similar to a "breaststroke" arm movement, does not require any kicking, and tends to be fairly effortless if you're calm.

Figure 3.6.4. Pop-up breath. Swimming along with double-arm sweeps, she pops up for air.

Calm bobbing can also be used in a horizontal position (for those who float horizontally) without any movement at all, save the one that it takes to come up and breathe. Bobs or pop-up breaths are wonderful to use in triathlon if you want to avoid the fray; it's possible to just hang out in a calm bob.

3.6.5 Rolling Over

Another way to get air easily, and perhaps the best-known safety move in triathlon, is to roll over like a sea otter from front to back. Once on your back, you can simmer indefinitely. Being on your back is a great place to rest and recover from common swimming issues, such as choking, foot cramps, leg cramps, and goggle malfunctions (see Section 4.2.2). From here, if you're calm, you can reboot your system while breathing as much as you want.

Eventually, you'll regain your breath and roll back over to your front to continue swimming. Remember, you don't want to be out there unless you are confident you can be calm.

There are two things about rolling that you need to know: protecting your nose, and "chop." By now, you already know to protect your nose when rolling from front to back or back to front by exhaling slowly though your nose.

"Chop" refers to choppy water. Being on your back may not work well if the water happens to be rambunctious from either nature or other human beings. In this case, bobbing or pop-up breaths facing away from the chop are fine options (Section 3.6.3 and 3.6.4). Either way, the air is there, and you can have all you want without working hard.

If you are fully present in your body when you come up for air in choppy water, you can feel its feedback telling you when it's safe to breathe (as in when your mouth is above the water as opposed to below it, and which direction to face), and you won't inhale water accidentally. If you are not calm and not present, that feedback is missed, and swimming in choppy water could get scary.

If you can propel yourself and roll over as we've described on both front and back while being in 1st Circle, you can swim in a triathlon from the start line to the finish line, with plenty of air to spare, without a single stroke of freestyle. We're not saying you'll break any Olympic records, we're just saying that it would work. Making it work is what's needed first, and speed can be added later. Remember the saying, "You can't swim a triathlon if you are afraid you might not live"? It was the living part that concerned you. And now that you've learned about the 1st Circle, you can resolve this.

Once you can be sure you will stay calm and can get all the air you want and that you will live, you can build a lovely freestyle if you wish.

3.7   Your Friend: Deep, Dark Water

If you felt yourself going out of the 1st Circle when you read that heading, it's worth noting. Deep water can be your friend if you're a Swimmer, and if you aren't, it can be scary. If you struggle with this fear, it is an indication you don't yet understand how the water and your body work together. This is a good realization, and it is important! To learn how the water and your body work together, digest and absorb the steps in this book.

Here's an interesting truth about deep water: in swimming, the depth is rarely used. Unless you're some kind of blue whale, tuna, or California kelp plant, you don't swim in the deep—you only swim in the top three or four feet of the water. The rest of that briny blue just supports you.

Deep Water Entries

In a few weeks or months, after you've mastered being in deep water—when you can float, rest, swim, and play at will—then it becomes safe to try an entry into deep water by jumping in. It might take some time to be able to even think about jumping into deep water. If you're not calm and don't think you can stay in the 1st Circle jumping into deep water, it's not time to try this skill, and it's definitely not time to do it in a race. Go back and spend time on all of the skills prior to this one. Do these until you have done them enough and own them. Then it will be exciting to try jumping in.

If you can stay calm and not move a muscle after jumping into deep water (and if you're a floater), something neat will happen. You will—in five or six seconds—descend as far as gravity takes you (three to five feet), stop descending, and float back up to the surface on your own. Would it be fun to hold your breath for six seconds and just wait to float up? It's not a fast trip to the surface, but your buoyancy *will* overcome the effect of gravity and you *will* slowly rise to the surface like froth in chicken soup.

Does this sound fun? If not, would it sound like more fun to do it with a spotter? If you don't want to descend very far, use your arms to slow and stop your descent at any point and propel yourself back to the surface. Feel. Stay with your body. Listen to your body.

For everyone, the higher the height from which you jump and the heavier and more streamlined you are, the deeper you'll go into the water. So, if you're a sumo wrestler jumping in from 20 feet above the water, you might want to be prepared with a large lungful (or two) of air! However, if you don't want to go that deep, spread your arms and feet to cause as much resistance as you can when you enter the water, greatly shortening your descent.

If you don't want to wait to float up, you can also propel yourself upward toward the surface by sweeping your arms downward. For floaters, the float will always bring you back to the surface, helped by the air in your lungs. If you don't have much air (but then, why wouldn't you?) or if you're a sinker, you can propel yourself back up to the surface. It doesn't take long to swim up, and it's not strenuous. Floaters: let yourself be helped by the water. Wait, feel it, and do what's needed. Sinkers: stay with your body and feel the power of your arm sweeps, one at a time. No one should jump in if they're not 100% sure they'll be safe.

You'll want to know you can stay calm while ascending in deep water. You don't want your body to be five feet under while your mind is at the surface! That's scary. Keep yourself with your body. If your body is underwater, stay in it. This is something to play with during practice and not during the first jump from the dock at a triathlon. When you know you can do this and stay in the 1st Circle, the triathlon dock jump sounds fun and not something to avoid or get past. The goal is to have zero parts of the triathlon that you need to "just get past." That first jump is critical to setting the stage for your entire event, so you owe it to yourself to be able to enjoy it.

Swimming in Deep, Dark Water

When it comes to dark water (water that isn't clear pool water or clear open water), the darkness has no impact on whether floating or propelling will work. What are your beliefs about dark water? Monsters? Sharks? The unknown? It may sound silly, but it's a legitimate question to ask yourself. What is it? Dark water can be surprising and disconcerting if it's new to you. It is caused by dark skies, depth, or dark-colored matter on the bottom. You will want to allow your resistance and not push past it. Feel it in your body. Sit with it. Give it permission to be there. This is not a time to be in a hurry. It will feel better if you listen.

If you do this, it is inevitable that slowly, you will become accustomed to darker water in places where you feel safe. Don't push or force yourself to encounter it in areas that make you even more nervous (deep water, for example). Also, for safety's sake, never jump into dark water if you don't know how deep it is and exactly what is there. There can be myriad things below the surface that aren't good for humans to encounter, such as sharp objects or a shallow bottom.

A good way to approach learning about yourself in dark water is to stand on the bottom at a beach or lake where you feel safe and check how you feel about putting your face into the water. It goes without saying that you should never swim alone, so bring a friend. If you don't want to put your face in, don't. Remember, we don't care if you put your face in; we care that you stay in the 1st Circle. If you can put your face in and remain calm for this, practice a front float there.

This kind of gentle progression is a fine way to approach getting used to dark water and remaining calm. If you push yourself to move forward when you're not calm, it will delay or prevent your progress. You always want to start in the 1st Circle and remain there. If you start to move toward the 2nd Circle, go back to the 1st and *keep practicing it.* We are not managing fear. We're healing it.

3.8   Fear of Not Being Able to do Freestyle

The definition of knowing how to swim has been confused with knowing how to do freestyle. People are sometimes afraid they can't do freestyle. But as we've said already, freestyle isn't what makes you safe.

It's important to take your time with the skills we've addressed, both the physical skills and that of staying in the 1st Circle. Sort out what is scary: the depth, darkness, or being unsure that you can stay in your body. Maybe it's all three, and that's okay.

When you commit to the 1st Circle first, you will be on your way to healing every part of your triathlon swim fear. As you know, safety means being in control of yourself. You are in charge of your own safety.

3.9 You Are Your Own Safety

By now you know that you're in charge of staying in 1st Circle. Therefore, you can learn to rely on yourself for your safety. Are you willing to do that by staying true to yourself all the time?

What are a few things that shouldn't be your sources of safety?

1. **Wetsuits.** If you happen to be wearing a wetsuit, its neoprene-powered buoyancy makes you a super floater. A wetsuit, however, does not make you safe. It's common for some triathletes to say they feel safer because their race has been deemed "wetsuit legal" at the last minute. Right away, you know these people aren't Swimmers, and that they don't yet fully understand or embody the messages in this book. A wetsuit keeps you warm and indeed it is quite buoyant, but it's not a safety device, and it has almost no bearing on whether your face stays out of the water or whether you panic.

2. **Kayakers and safety staff.** Triathletes often say they're glad kayakers and safety boats are nearby and available at races, and this is all well and good. However, a kayaker or a safety boat is not the basis for safety. You want to get your safety from yourself, right? In general, these vessels are there to watch over swimmers. It's fine that you enjoy having them there, and perhaps they help you stay in your body. But you are responsible for your own safety.

It's a sad fact that many instances of open-water deaths have occurred in triathlon. While most are ruled cardiac events, it's not often clear whether the cardiac event resulted in the drowning, or if the panic or fear of drowning caused the cardiac event, leading ultimately to drowning. Either way, one of the things you can control is keeping your body and mind calm . . . *by not biting off more than you can chew.* This prevents panic that can lead to further trouble.

3. **Safe behavior of other people.** You may be one of those who think, "I'm fine with just ME being in the water. It's not *me* that I'm afraid of, but rather all of the other yahoos swimming like manic sardines around me." This is a valid point, but was it not Confucius who said, "Don't let them dull your sparkle"? (Actually, no, it wasn't Confucius, but we think it's a pretty good quote). Anyway, the point is that no one can take your buoyancy, air, or presence of mind. The calm you possess when you know how to Swim is yours alone. Whether someone dings you with their elbow or inadvertently pushes you underwater, you as a Swimmer must know how the water works, how to prevent panic, how to find air reliably, and how to deal with unexpected water going down the wrong pipe. Trusting yourself in this regard will render you safe from the unwelcome arms and legs that may cross your path.

4. **Lack of aquatic life.** There may be some of you who say, "I'm fine with people, but what about those creepy crawly swimming things? *What if I get bitten by a shark, an alligator, or piranha?!?!*" Well, that all depends. Are you swimming in an area where these creatures swim? Even in these cases, the 5 Circles still apply, and you can decide whether you can stay in the 1st Circle knowing these animals could be present. Plenty of people do swim in these areas and take

precautions as well as risks.[5] Calm may not be an option for you under those conditions, and thus perhaps that particular event is not for you. The vast majority of triathlon races are not situated in areas where sea animals are considered to be a large factor, while a few race directors like the idea of adding another challenge (and a big legal waiver). Overall, fish generally don't want to be near humans and tend to avoid them, much like the frantic scattering that occurs when you put your hand into a fish tank. For alligators, that's not as true. The point is that you are the one in charge of staying calm in the 1st Circle, and you have the great privilege and responsibility of deciding which events are appropriate for you.

Regarding seaweed and aquatic plants, you also need to consider whether a race you're interested in is likely going to contain these plants, and ask yourself how you feel about them. Does their slipperiness and sliminess make you squeamish? Do you believe the plants' tendrils will entangle you and restrain you from getting air? Even though most near-shore plants don't have the physical properties to appreciably restrain a swimmer, if someone panics when in the presence of aquatic plants, that panic is dangerous to them. If you aren't ready to swim near plants while staying in the 1st Circle, it's not the race for you at this time. Again, your own control over staying in the 1st Circle, and trusting yourself will lead you to the right answer. Give yourself time to overcome your fear. It may take longer than you want it to, but your learning will transform your triathlon and augment every area of your life.

---

[5] Marathon swimmers Martin Strel, Diana Nyad, Lynne Cox, Steven Munatones, and countless others, e.g.

5. **Being fit.** Even the fittest people in the world aren't safe in the water if they don't understand how the water works and lack presence of mind in the water. Fitness is a factor which makes freestylers go faster or farther but has no bearing on the ability to Swim.

6. **Being tough.** There's a certain "tough guy" phenomenon in triathlon wherein well-meaning motivational messages often champion the attitude that triathletes have to be "tough." These messages give the advice that signing up for a triathlon when you're afraid of deep or open water is a great idea because it'll give you a chance to become tough and overcome your fear.

    We are saying the exact opposite. We're saying you should overcome your fear first so you can enter triathlons with complete confidence. It's important to recognize that tough-guy attitudes have not led to greater safety in triathlon; they have led to greater danger for some people. What leads to greater safety is knowing you should not enter a triathlon until you've overcome deep- and open-water fear. That shows true toughness. Everyone should avoid entering a triathlon for which they aren't likely to stay in 1st Circle for any reason. Besides, being the other "tough" doesn't make someone safe.

    What is toughness, anyway? The great triathletes are tough. They are well conditioned, they have good form, they work hard, eat well, have a habit of positive thinking, and are confident that they can take care of themselves. What makes them tough?

It's listening to their bodies; knowing when it's time to push and when it's not. Yes, they may force themselves to get up early. But that's not unsafe. They may force themselves to ride longer or run farther. But that's not unsafe. And if it is, they'll learn not to do it next time. You are learning not to take your life into your hands next time.

Triathletes are tough when they don't give up in the face of defeat; when the going gets rough and they hang in there; when their reserves can be called up at a time when they thought none were left; when they decide to do the right thing instead of the convenient thing; when they stay in the 1st Circle, even if it will cost them time, while others are "losing it." What is your definition of tough?

If you're thinking, "Okay, I've read this book, now I'm signing up for PlatinumMan in Acapulco. I have six months to get to calm," now is NOT the time to sign up. The time to sign up is when you *already* know that you can stay calm and the race sounds fun with regard to where you are *then*. Putting a deadline on your ability to stay calm will make you feel pressured and will only serve to put you into the 2nd or 3rd Circle as you train, and potentially on race day. You may even have to cancel and lose your entry fee. Save yourself money and heartache by following this advice!

Moreover, difficulties with safety in triathlon swims are usually due to two things: (1) athletes not knowing what they are getting into, and (2) athletes voluntarily taking safety risks.

Getting into these difficulties is not an example of good self-care. As mentioned previously, pushing yourself in the realm of swim fear leads to actions that are out of sync with your ability to stay calm. It's discouraging and defeating, and it *does not work* in the long term. The truth is that the wisest and most tough-minded thing you can do is to take time for yourself and heal your fear now. Then sign up for a triathlon once the swim sounds like fun AND it is safe for you.

Safety in triathlons is mandatory. You are the one who makes it so. Support such as kayaks, water staff, and swim tests are measures that race directors can choose in order to help racers self-select the appropriateness of a race for themselves. However, only you can make a good decision about the triathlons that are safe for you to enter: races where you can stay in the 1st Circle. You are in charge of your safety and happiness.

4

YOUR SWIMMING BELIEFS

You are now at the true/false section of this book. The right answer is always the one that is true for you. In the summary checklist and discussion of beliefs below, you might recognize yourself. See which beliefs you hold. Even if you don't have any of these beliefs, there is value in poking through them to bring to light ideas you have about the water.

Place a checkmark next to the beliefs you have. Then review what you've been learning in this book. If you think one belief sounds silly but you would act as though you believed it if you were in the situation, put a checkmark beside it.

Mind

____ I am the only nervous one.

____ Pushing through fear is the way to overcome it.

____ If I want to overcome fear in open water, I have to follow the coach's directions, even if I am afraid.

____ Sometimes I cannot keep my presence of mind in deep or open water.

____ My mind works differently in deep or open water than it does in the pool or shallow water.

____ I do not trust myself in deep or open water.

____ The concepts in this book may work for others, but they may not work for me.

Body

____ I am not a floater.

____ If I get splashed, I will get water in my nose or mouth, and I will struggle, sputter, cough, and possibly drown.

____ I need to be more physically fit to be safe.

____ Each breath I take must be maximal in case I don't get another one.

____ I cannot control my body well in deep or open water.

____ If I relax in deep water, I will either lose control or drop straight to the bottom like a stone; therefore, it is unwise of me to relax in water.

Skills

____ To float correctly, my body must be horizontal.

____ My ability to float depends on the depth of the water.

____ I cannot get air if I am in deep or open water because there is no bottom to stand on.

____ When I am in deep or open water, I must move vigorously to stay afloat.

____ Not moving equals drowning.

____ In deep water, I need skills that I don't need in shallow water.

____ In order to rest, I need the bottom or the side.

____ It is more difficult to get air in deep water than in shallow water.

____ I have to swim the whole distance using freestyle.

Water

____ Shallow water is as dangerous as deep water.

____ Shallow/deep water does not hold me up.

____ The water is more powerful than I am.

____ Cold water makes me panicky.

____ Wearing a wetsuit in the water makes me anxious.

4.1 Beliefs: Your Mind

Our beliefs determine how we react in situations both in and out of water. For this reason, let's start with the mind as we dive into our discussion of beliefs.

4.1.1 I am the only nervous one.

As previously mentioned, 46% of American adults are afraid in deep water, and 64% are afraid in deep open water. If you have open-water swim anxiety, you are part of a vast and invisible community. In triathlon, oftentimes the fear is looked upon as part of the athletic challenge, which—because it's water—is not only unfortunate, but debilitating and unsafe. Fear is not a given, or an expected part of triathlon. Swimming fearlessly can be a reality if you know how to prevent panic before it has a chance to start.

4.1.2 Pushing through fear is the way to overcome it.

Pushing through fear does not work for conquering anxiety in triathlon swimming. If it did, there would be no triathletes still afraid of the swim. And there would be no need for the large library of books and articles that deal with managing fear symptoms. Fear is not the problem, it is the symptom. The symptom appears when control is absent. The way to overcome fear is to start with—and stay in—a state of control, and move forward in control toward the next steps. You'll feel the excitement of competing, but you won't fear for your safety.

4.1.3 If I want to overcome fear in open water, I have to follow the coach's directions, even if I am afraid.

Some swim instructors don't know about the interplay between calmness and control, and they therefore overemphasize the importance of a technical freestyle. In the process of trying to do what instructors tell you, you may have ignored your own gut feeling that doing scary things is not a great idea when it involves the water. You may have been coached to do things that make you afraid. As you now know, no practice of fear or tense skills is going to move someone toward fearless swimming, or for that matter safer swimming.

4.1.4 Sometimes I cannot keep my presence of mind in deep or open water.

It may be true of you right now that you have a difficult time remaining mentally present in deep or open water. Therefore, go back to water where you can be fully present. Be honest and true to yourself. As you learn to slow down and stay true to yourself, you will learn how the water works, stay in the 1st Circle, prevent panic, and stay calm in deep, open water. This slowing down saves years of wasted time.

4.1.5   My mind works differently in deep or open water than it does in shallow water. I do not trust myself in deep or open water.

If that's true, could it be said that you keep your mind in shallow water and lose it in deep water? If your safety right now comes from relying on the wetsuit, pool bottom, wall, lane line, kayakers, boats, or luck, go back to water where you can trust yourself and be fully present. Be honest and true to yourself. The calm and control you are learning will expand.

4.1.6   The concepts in this book may work for others, but they may not work for me.

You will find out if you try it. If you are a human being, the 5 Circles apply to you. You are not the one exception. It takes time to learn, but not too much time. It saves far more time and years of painful triathlons. It may even save your life.

4.2   Beliefs: Your Body

4.2.1   I am not a floater.

Here's a good one! You may or may not be a floater. What is your definition of floater? The odds are great that you float. As discussed in Section 3.4, most people are floaters based on their muscle- and bone-to-fat ratio. It is only those who have very low body fat that tend to sink. If you are a floater, your float may take a different angle than someone else's. In a back float, your face may be the only part of you that's out of the water, but it is still a float, and it is good.

If you are a sinker, that is fine, as being a sinker does not remove your capacity to be a good Swimmer. Being a sinker just means that you'll need to scull slightly to stay at the surface, but if you are calm and in control, this will be something you can learn to do with ease.

4.2.2 If I get splashed, I will get water in my nose or mouth; I will struggle, sputter, cough, and possibly drown.

At some point or another, in the pool or in open water, you may have had the experience of having water splashed in your face that entered your nose, mouth, or both. While it can be uncomfortable for this to happen, water in the nose and mouth is not of itself a life-threatening moment. What turns a water-swallowing experience into an emergency is a lack of understanding of how it works, and panic.

Often, a panicked person will turn to treading water to try to get the head fully out of the water. However, the back float is a better way to recover because it requires so much less energy, and at the same time allows you to rest. You need a reliable, easy back float.

Remember BE-DO-HAVE. When you can *be* calm, knowing you can find air when you need it, you can *do* the movements required to get on your back with confidence, and you can *have* safety.

In open-water races, especially in saltwater, splashing and waves are common. In this case, being on your back might expose your face to more water. If this happens, letting yourself go into a vertical position for a few bobs might be just the solution to allow a cough (fun fact: you can cough under water) and to get air again, then resume swimming. Stay vertical until you have recovered. You may even want to swim a few strokes off to the side in less crowded water. Being present enables you to do these things.

If you aren't able to clear your goggles because there's sunblock or grease on them and you must remove them, remember that many people around the world swim without goggles. Swimming is not as comfortable without goggles, but it is possible. Try swimming without goggles in training. Let this be part of your preparation. If you practice it, it will not be a big deal if you have to ditch them. If you wear contacts, you can prevent a lot of goggle drama by wearing your goggle strap under your cap as extra protection so that they don't get nudged off.

Once you've done all of these things calmly in shallow water, you can practice them with others, and in deeper water. Remember that your learning will only progress if you are in the 1st Circle. If you practice nervousness and tension, it will not help you reach your goal of becoming confident and happy.

4.2.3   I need to be more physically fit to be safe.

You may believe you are not trained enough for your race distance. That may indeed be true, and triathletes should train fully with whatever stroke they intend to use in their race, with the option to change their minds any time. However . . .

Cardiovascular training and strength training do not equal safety.

It doesn't matter if you're the most fit, well-trained, efficient, beautiful freestyler in the world. If you're afraid in water over your head, you are not safe there because you don't have sufficient understanding of the water. Fitness is not relevant to knowing the water.

4.2.4 Each breath I take must be maximal in case I don't get another one.

If you're not sure where your next breath will come from, you'll feel the need to load up on air each time you get a chance. Uncertainty about getting air when you need it is the only sign you need to know you shouldn't be swimming in a triathlon. Yet.

It doesn't mean there's no hope. You need go back and fill in the missing steps.

4.2.5 I cannot control my body well in deep or open water.

You're reading this book because you have difficulty maintaining control in deep or open water. If you feel in control in a shallow-water lake but not in deep water, stay in the shallow and practice all of the swimming activities that you enjoy until you feel confident that the water holds you up and you know how the water and your body work together. Eventually, you'll want to try the next thing, which may be deeper water.

You might be saying, "But that's exactly the point. I *am* comfortable in shallow water, and I could do any triathlon if it were in shallow water where I can stand up!" True . . . but in that situation, your safety would come from the bottom and not from yourself. Train in shallow water in the lake, and when you need to rest, don't use the bottom.

If you've always needed the bottom to stay in control, your attention has been on the bottom and not in your body, where you control getting enough air and keeping water out of your nose.

The really great thing about relying on yourself for your safety is that whether or not the bottom is there, YOU AND YOUR

BODY always will be. Do you truly want to learn to prevent panic in the deep? Then pave a new road by calmly doing what you like in the shallow, exploring every nuance of it until you're so filled with it that you organically begin to try something new.

4.2.6   If I relax in deep water, I will either lose control or drop straight to the bottom like a stone; therefore, it is unwise of me to relax in water.

Have you tried it? You'd only want to try it if you felt safe that help was right there if you needed it. Do this in a pool, not open water. If you think you might lose control, do it in the shallow water, not the deep.

Whether you're a floater or a sinker, if you're not calm in the water, go to a safe depth and, while attempting to float, let the tension be there. Be sure to take care of your nose. Tension has a message for you. There's a belief that you're not safe. Listening to your body gives it a chance to inform you.

4.3   Beliefs: Your Skills

4.3.1   To float correctly, my body must be horizontal.
Please see Sections 3.5.2 and 3.5.3 for discussion on this.

4.3.2   My ability to float depends on the depth of the water.
Section 3.4 explored how floating is a result of your body's composition and your air. Scientifically speaking, your body will float in three feet, 33 feet, or 333 feet of water.

The location of the bottom may have some bearing on the angle at which you float. If the water is very shallow, your feet may touch the bottom because it gets in the way when your legs dangle down. If the water is deep, your feet won't touch. Either way, you still float.

4.3.3 I cannot get air if I am in deep or open water because there is no shallow bottom to stand on.

If standing up were the only option for getting air, then you would be absolutely right! But bobs, being on your back, and knowing how to Swim are the options when there is no bottom (Sections 3.5 and 3.6).

4.3.4 When I am in deep or open water, I must move vigorously to stay afloat. Not moving equals drowning.

Even sinkers can stay at the surface with gentle movements if they're present. No vigor required.

Seasoned swimmers don't work hard to stay up or stay safe. There is no question about staying afloat. Safety is a given. Because they don't think twice about it, their efforts can be focused on racing hard. Swimmers also don't take risks with their breath. They keep their breath comfortable at all times. They breathe hard while racing, but it feels completely safe and comfortable.

4.3.5 In deep water, I need skills that I don't need in shallow water.

The skill of staying in your body in the deep is the one you're missing at the moment. If you can stay in your body in the shallow without depending on the bottom for your safety, then you'll be ready—if it sounds like fun— to try staying in your body in the deep.

4.3.6   In order to rest, I need the bottom or the side.

At this point in your triathlon life, you may indeed need the bottom or the side to rest. It's okay. Once you learn how the water works, you will be able to float and bob to rest anytime you choose. Remain in control. It takes some personal power to slow down all the way to a stop and give yourself time to learn this. How much time? Two or three weeks of focused practice, typically.

4.3.7   It is more difficult to get air in deep water than in shallow water.

If your safety is rooted in using the bottom in the pool or lake, then yes, breathing will be easier when the bottom is close. On the other hand, if your safety is rooted in yourself, you can always get air at will.

Fear is what makes breathing difficult. If you feel tense or anxious, it's virtually impossible to coordinate your breath and movement. If you're calm and present, it will be obvious to inhale only when your face is above the water and not below—and how to get there.

4.3.8   I have to swim the whole distance using only freestyle.

As a triathlete, you may feel that somehow you are less of an athlete if you use a stroke other than freestyle. If you did, would you feel you hadn't proven your mettle? We know this sentiment is out there, but isn't it a mistake? To be a fast triathlete, you have to use freestyle because it's the fastest stroke. But you aren't a fast triathlete yet. Take the pressure off. Breaststroke and backstroke are viable strokes that do the job. Back floating and bobbing are valid ways any elite swimmer would use to take mental and physical rests if needed. Some should have taken rests and they didn't. If you have used floating and bobbing in races, consider being proud of yourself for honoring your feeling and trusting yourself to do what you needed to do. That is what safety is. Safety comes first. Keeping yourself safe restores self-trust and builds confidence.

If you want to swim freestyle, you can learn it. But it's not your next step. First you need to become happy and peaceful in open water. Remember, there are no race officials sitting with a pair of binoculars looking to tag people who aren't swimming freestyle. Plus, no matter how you finish, you still get a medal and a t-shirt. Your family and friends don't care if you swim freestyle. They would rather you be safe and reach the finish line to eat pizza with them. Please check your expectations of yourself and be sure they fit your level of experience and knowledge.

True, you may not be the top podium finisher if you stop frequently to float and rest. But by committing to the 1st Circle, YOU WILL BE SAFE, and you will have more fun. You have to be a living triathlete before you can be a fast one! You will extend the life of your triathlon career.

4.4   Beliefs About Water
Beliefs about water have a large bearing on how you approach your triathlon swims.

4.4.1   Shallow water is as dangerous as deep water.
Is it the water that's dangerous, or the person? Any water, shallow or deep, can be dangerous if a person is panicking. And it's true, some water is dangerous.

4.4.2   Shallow water/deep water does not hold me up.
If you are one of the few people who are sinkers, it's true that neither shallow nor deep water will hold you up by itself. Nonetheless, even sinkers, when calm, can learn to scull and provide lift for themselves to breathe and rest when they need to without tiring themselves out. When floaters are swimming, the

float holds them up. When sinkers are swimming, the lift created from their movements enables them to stay up.

4.4.3   The water is more powerful than I am.

In certain instances, water is more powerful than human beings or even boat motors. You can stand at the rim of the Grand Canyon and marvel at the rock that was weathered away by millennia of the Colorado River's flow. You can go to Hawaii and see the three- and four-story waves. You've no doubt heard about strong rip currents along ocean beaches in certain wind conditions.

At other times, the water is placid. Yet even if it's wavy, it can be perfectly benign. If it's scary at those times, then the lack of information may be more powerful than you, not the water. This need not persist!

Regarding currents, it goes without saying that most triathlon water currents are somewhere between the Colorado River and a glassy pond. In race waters, water velocity versus your propulsion determine your distance and speed. If you're swimming with great propulsion against a weak current, you'll make good progress. However, even strongly propulsive swimmers may not make much progress against a strong current.

Hence, as a triathlon swimmer, learn as much as you can about the potential current and wave conditions that you could face in your races. Doing so gives you a chance to see if you would enjoy swimming in the expected race conditions. Check with race directors and former competitors, and practice ahead of time with a spotter or kayaker in similar conditions. Be well informed and assess your readiness beforehand. No one wants to drive or fly 400 miles after having paid an $800 entry fee only to quit a panicky swim because they were not ready for the two-foot waves.

When evaluating a race in which you must swim against the current, you could make different decisions depending on the situation:

1. If you think swimming against the current is something that would make you leave the 1st Circle, then it's not time to sign up for that race. Wait until your swimming is at a point where it sounds like fun.

2. If swimming against the current sounds fun and you know you can stay in the 1st Circle, ask yourself whether your propulsive ability is greater than the expected current, and whether you can sustain it long enough to finish the swim. If you'll make limited progress against the race current, is it likely that you will eventually leave 1st Circle? It's good to think about these things ahead of time and to be in charge of your comfort! It's the more advanced triathlete who decides to stick with the races that seem fun rather than pushing into a race that's likely to turn scary. That will only defeat your self-trust and delay your progress.

3. If you do decide that you can beat the current and remain calm, fair enough. You've gone into the race with your eyes open.

You see, any of these decisions could be fine decisions. What is most important is that you stay true to yourself and honor what sounds fun.

Unless you're named Moses and lived several thousand years ago, you're not in control of the water's velocity or wave activity.

Whatever happens, you may not be in charge of where your body goes in the current, but you can still be in control of your presence and your actions.

4.4.4   Cold water makes me panicky.

Interestingly, water temperature has a significant effect on how we experience swimming. While a nice warm bath or hot tub relaxes you, cool water may elicit a slight inhale and shiver, while even chillier water may make you feel jumpy and out of breath. In addition, think about the words used to describe fear: clammy hands, cold feet, having the shivers, goosebumps—words we use to describe feeling cold. *Fear is cold.*

Anxiety may feel more intense in a cold-water environment, which is one of the reasons it's helpful to learn about the water in warm pools (88 degrees Fahrenheit and above). If you're aware ahead of time that a triathlon will have cold water and that it will make you feel panicky, now is not the time to sign up for that race.

There are certain triathlons that have extremely cold water (55 degrees Fahrenheit and below), and cold-water acclimation to those more extreme temperatures is not a subject addressed in this book. However, no matter the water temperature, it is not the temperature that leads to panic. It is the ability to remain in 1st Circle that matters. You are responsible for staying in 1st Circle, and once you learn how, you can be in control, even if you're cold.

4.4.5   Wearing a wetsuit in the water makes me anxious.

Many triathletes don't wear their wetsuit enough before race day to be comfortable in it during a race. The newness of the wetsuit combined with the tightness of the neoprene (rubber) in the neck and chest area may mimic the chest tightness of panic. The unusual buoyancy afforded by the neoprene makes swimming feel wobbly. The wetsuit is often then unzipped or partially peeled off by inexperienced athletes, which creates high drag. The swimmer attempts to swim against high drag and becomes tired.

All of these things about wetsuit swimming are true at first: wetsuits are tight, new buoyancy is weird, and cold water has effects on the body. But you can acclimate to each of them so that they no longer throw you off center. It takes commitment to practicing with them and exposing yourself to various race conditions to ensure a safe, fun swim.

One work-around for easing the tightness of a wetsuit is to put it on in the water instead of on land. It's much easier in the water. Once you have it on, float in it. Float on your front and back. What changes in your position does the wetsuit cause? What effect does the cold have? Learn all these things *long* before a race. If you feel as though you might leave the 1st Circle soon, back up and go no further until it's fun. If you do this, you will calmly and inevitably progress to an increasing variety of scenarios in which you can race. This is how you heal your fear of being in a wetsuit. It's not the wetsuit that is the problem; the problem is not understanding how these things work (fear, wetsuits, water).

5

HAPPY TRIATHLON FREESTYLE

This book teaches you how to derive your swim safety from *yourself* instead of relying on the bottom, the side, a wetsuit, strokes, or a boat. Once you are peaceful in water over your head, you can then examine the *choreography* of swimming in order to go faster: strokes, designed for efficiency in the water. Choreography is irrelevant to healing fear.

It is essential to focus for the majority of this book on the building blocks of confident swimming. Only when you ensure your own safety is happy, calm freestyle possible.

If you're just opening the book to this chapter, you missed the prize. Go back and spend time understanding the essence of this book. If you jump to freestyle without the rest of the book, you won't get what you want. Having a better freestyle cannot fix triathlon swim fear.

The next sections are not part of overcoming fear. We include them because once you do overcome your fear, they're important to know . . . and we don't want to wait until our next book to tell you about them!

5.1   Free Freestyle: Race Day Basics

Free: now doesn't that just sound like a lovely place to be?

Floating on the breeze . . . cruising along like a barge . . .

Wait, a BARGE?

Well, that's how some triathletes feel when swimming freestyle. Like a giant barge overcoming tons of resistance. That's not the most relaxing or efficient way to swim. There are key stroke techniques that can help turn that wide, unwieldy barge into a sweet, sleek kayak. Once you've mastered the 5 Circles and you trust yourself for your safety, your freestyle can be truly free.

5.1.1   Horizontal Body

When floating, your body position in the water is determined by your buoyancy. If you float diagonally, you wouldn't want to remain diagonal as you swim down the pool. Your speed while swimming lifts you from diagonal to horizontal. But there are fine points to learn that take you from being horizontal and inefficient to horizontal and efficient.

You want to be in the best position to slide through the water.

Remember the prone float from earlier in Section 3.5? This float is like a see-saw. If your head is up, your feet go down. If your head is down, your feet go up (a little). Your head is the most important part. Imagine pushing off of the wall with your arms out in front of you and your legs behind you, using a gentle kick to keep your feet near the water's surface. Keep a "neutral head," which is to say that your neck is relaxed and the back of your head is in line with your spine. You're looking straight down at the bottom. Even slightly lifting your head causes the other side of the see-saw to drop (your hips), which results in undesirable drag or resistance through the water.

As you begin to stroke freestyle, become aware of your line of vision—is it pointing straight down? If not, you are unknowingly lifting your head. Make an adjustment, and you will be able move through the water more easily.

5.1.2   Rolling to Breathe: Side Breathing

Think about how you may have done side breathing in the past. If you tend to choke or inhale water frequently, you may have been inhaling while your mouth was still under water. Do you agree that if you're inhaling while your mouth is under water, you might not be all "there?"

Recall the action of rolling from front float to back float (Section 3.6.5), and how it enables you to breathe at will. When swimming freestyle and learning to get a reliable breath, practice rolling all the way over onto your back to guarantee that your mouth will clear the water. To keep you in the 1st Circle, you must guarantee air. Just do this for a few days until you feel absolutely confident that you'll get air, not water, every single time. You must have certainty.

Drill: When swimming freestyle, leave one arm out front while rolling over onto your back. You will have one arm out front and one at your side after you've rolled over. On your back, float (if you're a floater) or scull with one hand (if you're a sinker) and take a nice, comfortable breath. Then, in one motion, roll back over onto your front and continue stroking with the arm that was at your side (Figure 5.1.2) The point is to stay horizontal in the water while getting air. You want to remain horizontal because it's less tiring and it is the best position to be in to resume swimming. Eventually, you won't need to roll all the way to your back. But until you're certain you will find air, do this to guarantee it. This builds confidence.

Figure 5.1.2. Rolling side breaths.

Now for a side story about parallel parking. Random? Maybe not! Remember when you learned how to parallel park and wanted nothing to do with other cars near you? You wanted the largest slot you could find with the oldest, junkiest cars in front of you and behind you. When you got better at it, you were more comfortable with maybe a mid-90s minivan to the front and a small sedan in the back. As you became more comfortable, you didn't mind parking in smaller slots with some nicer cars in front and behind (especially if you found rock star parking right next to your restaurant). Your ability to fit your car into the space improved as you became more confident with your parking skills. That's how breathing is in freestyle. The more certain you are that you'll find air every single time, the more comfortable you'll become in not rolling completely onto your back. That's when good side breathing becomes a possibility. If you work toward a side breath in this way, you will get to keep your wonderful horizontal body position *and* breathe easily. Choose comfort before technique.

In open-water situations, the rolling breath can be extremely helpful, especially in choppy water, since on your back, your mouth is even farther away from the water when you breathe. Also, if you decide you need to rest for a while, you're already on your back.

5.1.3   Light Kick

There are several reasons why kicking lightly can be helpful as you start to figure out a freestyle that works for you. The first reason is that kicking hard is detrimental. The second reason is that kicking hard is detrimental. Ha!

First, it's not necessary to kick hard to stay atop the water, as your float will do that for you (for floaters). Sinkers can kick gently to achieve the same end. If you're kicking hard, you're working too hard, using far too much energy. Is it possible that you still have the belief that you have to kick to stay up?

Second, swim physicists have found that while kicking requires a great deal of energy, it produces a rather small proportion of the overall swimming propulsion (10-12%; 27% in some elite sprinters[6]). This means that a super strong kick doesn't provide you with much forward propulsion. In addition, your large quadriceps muscles gobble up precious oxygen. You'll have an easier freestyle if you kick gently with slightly bending knees and floppy ankles, which is just enough movement to keep your legs where they need to be.

---

[6] Maglischo 2003, as cited in Taormina 2014.

5.1.4   Arm Movements

Because many people think a key to comfortable freestyle is the mechanics of arm movement, a lot of time and energy is spent discussing perfect freestyle arm form. But are the mechanics of the arms the key component to a good freestyle? No. *Calm* is the key. Once a swimmer is calm, the proper arm movements do make freestyle easier and faster—but not until calm has been attained.

There are many kinds of freestyle arm actions available to you, from windmill actions to those that make you look like an airplane about to take off from a runway. However, as long as your arms are moving as "one arm, then the other," you'll be able to get where you're going just fine. As you become more relaxed with your freestyle body position and breathing and become interested in being more efficient and going faster, you can spend some time with a coach, watch some online videos, and read some fun books about freestyle arm and pull paths.[7]

5.2   Race Day

Race day is where it all comes together. All of the practice you've done in the pool, in your mind, and in open water pays off here.

You can stand on the start dock and laugh with your friends. You can watch the sunrise and appreciate the swish of the waves and the call of the shorebirds. You can joke about how you look in that dorky suit and worry about whether you have time to go to the restroom one more time or not, and you can obsess about making sure your timing chip is still on your ankle.

---

[7] Refer to Sheila Taormina's *Swim Speed Secrets* series (VeloPress.com), as well as Terry Laughlin's *Total Immersion* resources (totalimmersion.net).

The one thing you won't be doing is worrying about whether you'll live or die. And losing that worry is the best feeling in the world.

5.2.1   No New Things on Race Day

The most well-worn adage in endurance sports is "nothing new on race day." This means it's unwise to do or wear anything new on the day of the triathlon. It's good advice, and it's especially important in swimming. One way to head straight to the 3rd Circle is to throw yourself curveballs you can't catch.

Commit to "nothing new on race day." Practice wearing your wetsuit at least five times prior to race day, learning what it feels like to wear it, and how it affects your mind and body (see Section 4.4.5). Practice your sunblock application. Wear your goggles in the same temperature water before race day and practice defogging them, taking them off, and putting them on in the water so you can know how this affects you. What if your hands are greasy? Avoid it! If the race requires you to wear a swim cap, practice wearing one to see how it feels.

A big piece of the preparation for triathlon swimming is to try to think of all of the scenarios for gear and location that you possibly can, and practice them in your training. If you can't prepare by practicing them, you'll at least have thought them through in theory.

Part of the reason pro triathletes are pros is because they've practiced and rehearsed in their minds ad nauseum all the little details that add up to a good race, and they have thought through all of the scenarios that may occur. They have a plan. Sometimes bad races happen: the weather was too hot, or they accidentally dropped their water bottle during the bike . . . but at least they were prepared from the outset.

5.2.2   Sighting

Sighting can be accomplished in several ways, including lifting the top of your head and looking forward as you come up to breathe. If lifting your head while swimming is complicated for you, or if you inhale water when you try to sight, you're ahead of yourself. Slow down, pilgrim! Another way to sight is to stop and use a bob or two to pop your head above the water and check your direction. Bob until you're certain you have a lock on your target.

If you prefer lifting your head to sight, there's a wonderful swim drill you can do called "head-up swimming" or "Tarzan swimming." This will strengthen your neck and upper shoulders for race day. To do this, swim freestyle with your head above the water for a few strokes, and then resume normal swimming. In just a few moments, you can see how much power this takes, and how helpful it can be to strengthen your neck as well as practice going from a diagonal to horizontal body position while swimming. Being a strong Tarzan swimmer can also be useful when navigating around triathlon buoys.

5.2.3   Starting and Finishing

As anyone who's ever seen the start of a triathlons will tell you, it can be a zoo when the gun goes off in a mass start. Some race directors are working to phase out the mass start in favor of a rolling or staggered start, but even in shorter races with a large starting group, you might feel like you're part of the zoo effect. The truth is that you don't have to start with all of those wild animals. Let the field go past. Waiting ten seconds to start can reduce the work you have to do without significantly impacting your finish time.

You can also start to the left or right of the main group of swimmers. Suppose the race course says you are to keep the buoys on your left. If there's a mass of people starting in the water or on the beach, you can start to the far right. This means that when you start swimming toward the buoys, most of the other swimmers will be ahead of you and will reach the first buoy just before you do. You'll also be swimming at a very slight angle toward them, which gives you more control at your angle of approach.

Once you finish your swim, you'll be looking for that lovely paragon of joy, the finish buoy. It's good to know what you're looking for when that happy moment arrives. You can help yourself prepare for this by getting into the water before the race starts (if race directors allow a warmup time) and looking back toward the finish line so that you recognize your mark. Even though it is possible to spot the finish from the beach or dock, there's nothing like being there at the level of the water to choose landmarks and secure your sights for the finish.

5.3   Swim Forth and Prosper

Triathlon swim fear can be healed. By following the advice offered in this book, you'll put yourself on a certain path to achieve it. From the 5 Circles to the freestyle stroke, let these concepts simmer in your brain and body. Then, if it sounds like fun, put them in the pool and open water (always with a buddy), and do it with enjoyment and peace of mind.

Most of all, know that swimming can be the most fun part of your triathlons—an experience you can look forward to with a thrill every time. Conquer your fear of triathlon swimming and end the dread by keeping the 1st Circle first.

FIGURES & REFERENCES

Dash, Melon. *Conquer Your Fear of Water; Learn to Swim with the 5 Circles, A Breakthrough in Teaching and Learning.* Brooklyn Writers' Press, 2020. Second edition.

Magslischo, Ernest. *Swimming Fastest.* Champaign, IL: Human Kinetics, 2003.

Taormina, Sheila. *Swim Speed Strokes.* Boulder, CO: Velo Press, 2014.

ABOUT THE AUTHORS

M. Ellen ("Melon") Dash is founder of Miracle Swimming School for Adults, which opened in Berkeley, CA, in 1983. She discovered and developed a new teaching paradigm that virtually guarantees that adults who are afraid in water will overcome their fear and learn to swim. It is accomplished with the "science of having fun." She wrote the book *Conquer Your Fear of Water*, produced the DVD *The Miracle Swimmer*, hosted *The Learn to Swim Show* on internet radio and has contributed game-changing concepts to the aquatics industry that have begun to have a global bearing on water safety. Dash has trained instructors around the world to use her teaching system. Her work has been featured in the *New York Times*, *Wall Street Journal*, *USA Today*, NBC's *Today* show, NPR, *Psychology Today*, *Athletic Business*, *Aquatics International*, *Recreation*, The Travel News Network, CNN's *Headline News*, *Real Simple*, and many others. Dash is world-ranked in three events as a U.S. Masters swimmer, and resides full time in Sarasota, Florida.

www.miracleswimming.com
www.melondash.com
melon@miracleswimming.com

Alicia ("Ali") Meeks is a lifelong swimmer, a former NCAA Division 1 collegiate athlete, and a three-time Ironman triathlon finisher. Following a successful career as a marine biologist, she founded ReadySetSweat, LLC, a company providing swim instruction and triathlon coaching. Meeks' swimming and open-water experience has rendered her a highly sought-after coach, from beginning swimmers to those refining their speed skills. She has been roundly praised for her ability to bring fun and excitement to the learning process for both children and adults. Meeks is a Licensed Miracle Swimming Instructor, a Red Cross/CPR Trained Lifeguard, a Certified Personal Trainer with the American College of Sports Medicine, a USA Triathlon Level 1 Coach, and a Training Peaks Certified Level 2 Coach. Meeks is active in her local triathlon community, volunteering and participating annually in open water and triathlon swims ranging to 10 miles. She lives in north Alabama with her husband, two out-of-control bird/couch dogs, and four good horses.

readysetsweat.net
trainer.ali.meeks@gmail.com

Made in the USA
Columbia, SC
02 July 2020